GOLF
STATE OF MIND

By David MacKenzie

Contents

Why Your Game is About to Improve and How to Use This Program 1

Technical Skills Do Not Equal Performance Skills 1
A Deep Dive into Sport Psychology and
Human Performance Training 4
It's Time for A More "Holistic" Approach 7
How To Use This Program 9

Module 1: Self Discovery 11

Your Vision and Beliefs 11
Your Purpose and Motivation 15
Your Player Identity Statement 16
Mindset 18
    A Fixed or Ego Mindset 20
    A Growth or "Mastery" Mindset 22
    A Competitive Mindset 29
Assessing Your Mental Game 30

Module 2: The Performance Process 31

Outcome Goals 32
Defining "Process" 36

Why Process Focus Improves Performance 36
The Phases of Performance 39
The Mental Scorecard 40
Being Present and Directing Attention 42

Module 3: The Shot Routine 45

The Phases of The Shot Routine 45
The Goals Of The Pre Shot Routine 47
Step 1: Switching on your "golf brain" 48
Step 2: The Planning Phase 49
Step 3: The Rehearsal Phase 54
    Visual Rehearsal or "Visualization" 55
    Physical Rehearsal 61
    Auditory Rehearsal 62
    Verbal Rehearsal 63
Step 4: Set Up and Alignment 63
Step 5: The Athletic Phase 66
    The "Athletic Mind" 66
    Breathe! 69
    Your Walk into the Ball 70
    Make it Quick and Reactive 70
    Target Retention and Visualization 71
    Being Aware of Tension 72
    Focus on Your Breathing 73
    Focusing on Feel 74

    Focusing on Sound/Tempo 74

    Using Words or Action Phrases 75

    Counting 76

    "Quiet Eye" 76

    Physical or "Kinesthetic" Swing Cues 78

Step 6: The Shot 79

    Types of Swing Thoughts 80

    External Focus...82

    Internal Focus 83

    Learning Style and Personality Traits....................85

    Kinesthetic Focus 87

    Auditory Focus 88

    Using Words during the swing 89

    Swing Thoughts Under Pressure 89

    Neutral swing thoughts...90

    Self-coaching and Making Adjustments................90

Step 7: The Post Shot Routine 91

    Accepting "bad" shots 92

    Choosing A Response Instead of Reacting............93

Module 4: Playing Fearless Golf 98

What is Fear? 99

    Fear of What Others Think...................................99

    Fear of Failure..101

In The Moment Fear 101
What Are Your Fears? 102
The Two Minds 102
    The Conscious Mind 104
    The Subconscious Mind 104
Reducing Pervasive Fear 109
    Changing Thinking Patterns 109
    Visualization to Overcome Fear 112
    Self Awareness or "Mindfulness" 114
    Mindfulness Meditation 118
    Focus 122
    Positive Psychology 122
Reducing "In The Moment" Fear 128
    Controlling Arousal 128
    Slow Down 139
    Visualization To Change Internal State 140
    Self Talk 141
    Body Language 149
    The Alter Ego Effect 151
    Anchors and Triggers 156
    Returning To The Present 161
    Practicing For Pressure 164
    Keep Expanding Your Comfort Zone 169

Module 5: Pre-Round Preparation and Warm-Up 172

Know The Course and Have a Strategy 172
Treat all rounds the same 175
Lower Your Expectations 176
Be Intentional 178
Recovery and Sleep 179
Eat and Drink Well 180
Get Your Equipment Prepared 181
Your Mental Game Warm-Up 182
    1. Breathe and Relax 182
    2. Be Grateful 183
    3. Visualize 184
    4. Activate Your Player Identity 186
    5. Play Music 187
Your Physical Warm-up Routine 188
    Putting Warm-up (15 mins) 188
    Short Game Warm-up (15 mins) 189
    Driving Range Warm-up (20 mins) 189
Module 5 Exercises 192

Module 6: Post-Round Reflection 193

Using A Performance Journal 194
A Simple Post Round Review 194

Scoring Your Mental Game 198
Stats to Record..202
Module 6 Exercises 203

Module 7: Planning and Executing 204

The Goal Setting and Achievement Process 205
    External Goals...206
    Internal Goals 208
    Taking Inventory and Setting Your Goals............209
    Process Goals or "The Tasks" 213
    Create A Two Week Plan ("The System")............214
    Using Visualization in Goal Setting.....................221
Golf and The Parallels with Life 224

Why Your Game is About to Improve and How to Use This Program

Firstly, I'd like to congratulate you on being open minded enough to explore game improvement techniques, which go beyond working on your swing.

I'm going to assume that you believe you are a better player than your scores would sometimes suggest, or that perhaps you know that your mind can get in the way of your skills but you don't know what to do about it. Perhaps you're a competitive player who feels the pressure to perform and struggles in tournaments?

Conversations I have with new students can often start like this: *"If you saw my swing, you'd think I was a scratch handicap, but I can't break 80!"* or *"On the range, I can hit any shot I want, but on the course it's a different story…"*

I'm sure that you're experiencing something similar, or at least you are aware that your performance on the golf course goes beyond how good your swing is.

Technical Skills Do Not Equal Performance Skills

I was there myself. Fifteen years ago, I was a competitive amateur golfer living in San Francisco, CA.

Having taken a break from the game whilst I lived and worked in London after graduating from the University of St. Andrews in Scotland, I found myself quickly regaining my passion for the game. I played in most of the weekend amateur tournaments I could find in the Bay Area, of which there were plenty. I worked hard on the technical aspects of my game - recording swing videos at the range and taking a weekly lesson. My swing had never felt or looked better. During my practice rounds, I would comfortably shoot around par. However, when it came to tournaments, it was a lottery which player would show up. On some days, I was able to play the golf I knew I was capable of, but on others, a different player would show up - an anxious, frustrated player who had something to prove to himself and others. On those days, the skills that I had displayed just days before were nowhere to be found. I was left searching and "playing golf swing", instead of playing golf. It had me scratching my head and wondering why there was such a gap between what I knew I could do and what was happening on the course.

Looking back, it is easy to identify what was happening – I was in my own way. Because I cared deeply about how I performed in tournaments, there were mental and physical changes that were preventing me from freely accessing my skills.

Like most golfers at the time, I wasn't ready to admit that it could be something "mental" that was causing me to struggle with shots that I could hit with ease in practice.

My ego and ignorance of the mental aspects continued to prevent me from solving the problem – it was much easier to tell myself: *"my swing was off that day"*, than to tell myself that mentally I wasn't strong enough.

During the time I lived in San Francisco, I became very interested in personal development and self-mastery. I wanted to discover how to achieve greater wellbeing, self-fulfillment and better performance in all areas of my life. As I read many books on Buddhism, Eastern Philosophy, Ancient Wisdom (such as Stoicism), Spirituality and more modern books such as Stephen Covey's "7 Habits of Highly Successful People", I couldn't help but relate much of what I was reading to my inconsistencies on the golf course and so I began to explore it further.

I realized that many of the principles in these books could not only help me develop the mental skills and strategies to be more productive and happier, but they could also benefit my golf game.

At that time there were very few resources to help me improve my "mental game of golf", compared to the vast libraries of books and videos on how to improve your golf swing. The few books that I did find on the subject were mostly full of anecdotes and contained little in the way of practical application and training.

None of the golf professionals I saw talked about it as being a factor in my performance. Here's my take on why:

1. The Golf Industry as a whole, makes money from selling swing lessons, equipment and training aids, which it promotes via TV, websites and magazines

2. Technical instruction is more tangible - you can immediately see the effects of a swing or equipment change. Changing the mental side of the game is a slower process and requires players (and coaches) to look deeper at themselves and be more vulnerable, which isn't as easy or as fun to do
3. Most golfers want quick fixes. Look at the front cover of any golf magazine and that's clearly what sells. Changing mindset and skill development is a longer-term investment, which requires more patience and discipline
4. Most golf instructors don't know how to teach the mental side of the game, nor do many of them buy into how much it improves performance, so they don't pass it onto their students

From the research I've done since, I believe that a lack of awareness, understanding and coaching available to improve the mental game and how we develop skill, is the main reason why the average handicap of 16 has not fallen during the past 50 years (this statistic is even more surprising when you consider how much clubs, balls and coaching tools have evolved in that time)

A Deep Dive into Sport Psychology and Human Performance Training

To learn more about how I could improve my mental game, it was clear that I would have to go beyond the sport of golf and look deeper into sport psychology and human performance training.

To begin my research, I wanted to get answers to the following questions:

> *Do elite performers in any field share a similar mindset and mental traits? If so, could these traits be learned or were they inherent talents?*
>
> *What techniques do Sport Psychologists use with their clients?*
>
> *How does an average golfer train and what is their mental approach during their rounds compared to elite level players?*
>
> *What exactly is "The Zone" or "Flow State"? Is it a random occurrence or do we have some control over it? What mental and physiological conditions are being met that allows such freedom and focus?*

As I researched these subjects and interviewed many golfers, performance coaches and Sport Psychologists, I was able to implement strategies and change my mindset to play with less ego, fear and judgment and my scores improved considerably.

The more improvement and enjoyment I experienced, the more I felt compelled to share my discoveries with other players. For this reason, I purchased the domain name "Golf State of Mind.com" and began writing a blog.

Because there was very little on the web regarding improvement of the "mental game of golf" at that time, my blog quickly got interest and positive feedback - it was helping other players lower scores and enjoy the game more. This inspired me to research further and produce more content, which eventually led to the creation of "The Golf State of Mind Training Program", which you are now using.

The program you are about to begin is far from the first iteration. The journey to untapping our human potential never ends, and I am still learning about myself and how to help others. Every day that I coach is a learning opportunity for me, and as such, the coaching program continually evolves to reflect that.

What started as a project to improve my own game has become my passion and purpose – not only to help golfers understand more about what brings out the best in them on the golf course, but off it too.

I've now helped hundreds of thousands of golfers lower their handicap, enjoy the game more and discover more about themselves for overall greater wellbeing.

Becoming the best that you can be requires looking just as much at yourself and how you are playing "the inner game", as it does your technical skills. However, when you look inside, you might find things that you don't want to see or admit. A swing change is easier, more tangible and doesn't require you to be vulnerable. But the "Inner work" is necessary for you to understand yourself and what you need to change so you can navigate the challenges ahead and fully express your talents.

Although I call this a "program", it's a player-centric approach. Everyone *will* benefit from implementing and practicing all 7 modules, but many of the concepts within them are for *you* to experiment with, test and reflect upon and build your own "process". We are all different in how we learn, communicate, and see the world, so it's important to find out what works best for you.

It's Time for A More "Holistic" Approach

Fortunately for all golfers, the golf industry is beginning to pay more attention to the benefits of a more "holistic approach", instead of solely focusing on a player's technique to improve their performance. More and more players (of all levels) are working on developing all the following 4 key skill sets:

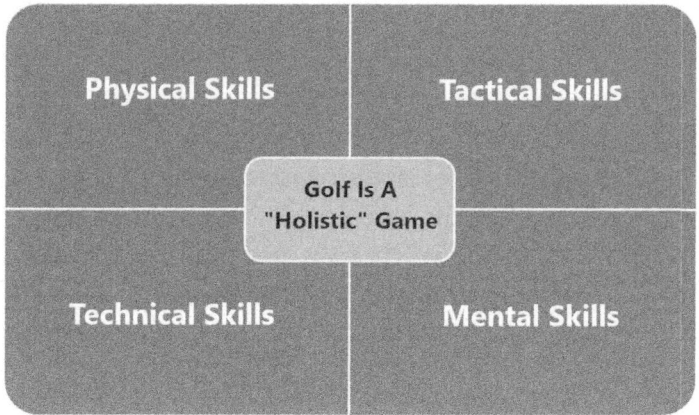

Physical skills:
Fitness, strength and conditioning, sleep, good nutrition

Technical skills:
Fundamentals, learning how to swing the club to hit different shots

Tactical Skills:
Golf I.Q. and Course Strategy. Knowing your game and the optimal shot to play given the situation/conditions

Mental or "Performance" skills:
Being able to focus on what brings out the best in your performance while removing limiting inhibitions

The Goals for this Training Program:
- Improve your mindset so that you approach problems with less "ego" and more curiosity
- Identify what brings out the best in you in each stage of a round (process goals)
- Develop strategies to deal with setbacks and control your "performance state"
- Learn how to measure your success in ways that go deeper than score and lead to long-term change for the better
- Practice in a way which challenges you to solve problems and develop skill, not just work on technique

Transferable Skills
"Golf is the closest game to the game we call life. You get bad breaks from good shots; you get good

> *breaks from bad shots, but you have to play the ball where it lies."*
>
> **- Bobby Jones**

In this system, we're going to discover what it is that brings out the best in you on the course, but you'll also find tools for personal growth and self-development in all areas of your life. We call it "the mental game of golf", but it may as well be called the "mental game of life". The mental skills required to access any of your skills more easily and deal with challenges are no different to those needed to play your best golf. If you can improve your ability to deal with pressure, focus, respond and not react, stay present, bounce back, view mistakes objectively, set goals, and gain a more positive, optimistic attitude, then you're improving valuable "human skills" which will help you achieve more success and fulfillment. The greatest gift that the game of golf can give you is not the trophies or scores, it's the life lessons it teaches you about yourself. Let's get to work!

How To Use This Program

Throughout each module, there are exercises to help with your understanding and building your mental skills and framework. Reading/listening to the material is important, but you need to engage with it to make real change.

For this reason, I recommend that you have a dedicated Golf State of Mind notebook ready to write notes and completedo the exercises. There is also additional reading and studies for the modules, which you can find at www.golfstateofmind.com/module-additional-reading

Module 1: Self Discovery

> *"Winners have learned to know themselves intimately"*
> — Dennis Waitley, author of "The Psychology of Winning"

In this module, you're going to do some self-discovery. Without knowing who you are and who you want to become, you won't be able to grow towards it.

Your Vision and Beliefs

> *"In order to be successful you have to develop your inner vision. If you have no vision for the future, you are destined to fail in the long run."*
> — Greg Norman

Why have a vision?
Before starting any journey, you need to have a destination in mind. We only get one shot at life, and our time is limited. Every day is precious and gives us the opportunity to create a better life for ourselves and others and bring our goals and dreams towards us. Time is never to be wasted or taken for granted. But without knowing where you want to go and what you value most, you can easily become stagnant and lose the

opportunity. With a long-term goal in mind, it directs your limited time and energy to taking steps towards it each day.

What does *your* future look like? Let's think about what is possible for you and create a vision of it. Make this a "dream goal". That way, if you fall short, you'll still achieve more than if you had set goals for something that is probable, or likely. The most successful people in any field didn't get there by setting goals that were realistic or expected. Instead, they aimed to do something extraordinary and then they figured out how to make it happen.

Once you have your vision, I'd like you to strip out the title of your achievement, whether it's winning a major, becoming world number one or winning the club championship and look deeply at the player you will have become. That's what we're aiming for, not the title or the award. If you make your goal about a title, or believe that winning a tournament such as the club championship will make you fulfilled, what happens after that? If instead, we make success about the values we want to cultivate and skills we want to develop, success and winning go deeper. When success is not measured by external results and where we finish, we are more in control of it, and we can perform with more freedom. Of course, I would like my students to win as much as possible, but we do this by making the player that we want to become the goal. I like to instill in my students that there's no such thing as a "big tournament" or "big round", they are all big! Thinking in this way helps you develop high performance habits and uphold your values in *every* moment, not just ones you consider "big".

How will it *feel* to have become who you want to be?

Make it a goal to visualize your "vision" a few times per week. When you see it repeatedly in your mind, it will cause you to think and act more in line with your values and increase motivation and effort.

Belief

"The biggest difference I've noticed between successful people and unsuccessful people isn't intelligence or opportunity or resources. It's the belief that they can make their goals happen."
– James Clear, Author of Atomic Habits

The path to your goals will be full of obstacles, and to keep pushing forward, you'll need to believe that you can eventually get there. *Why* do you believe that you can achieve your goals? What are the things that you do well and the characteristics you have that give you an indication that you have what it takes?

Limiting Beliefs

"Beliefs have the power to create and the power to destroy."
– Dr. Ken Ravizza

Having a vision of your dream goals (and visiting it regularly) is an important factor in you getting there.

But it would be naïve to think that the journey will be easy, and you won't be challenged by mental and physical obstacles along the way.

Let's think about the mental obstacles you will face, so you can prepare to deal with them. It's not being negative to think of what your limiting beliefs are, as you will need to change them at some point. Examples of limiting beliefs are:

> *"Better players are born with more talent"*
> *"I don't have as much time as other people"*
> *"I can't afford the best coaching"*
> *"These fields are too strong"*
> *"The other players are much more confident that I am"*
> *"I'm not good enough to make the team"*
> *"I always get in my own way when I have a chance to go low"*

We'll work on challenging and changing these limiting beliefs later in the program.

Vision Exercises:

In your notebook, write your answers to the following questions:

1. What is your vision? Write down and create an image in your mind for your short-term (1-3 years) and long-term (5-10 years) vision
2. How will it feel to achieve these goals?

3. Why do you believe that you can achieve these goals? Write down all your best qualities
4. Do you have any limiting beliefs that are holding you back from becoming the player you want to be?

Your Purpose and Motivation

*"When I was a young player, I had no visions in my head of fans and trophies. I basically sought 3 things from the game: To **improve** at it, to **compete** at it and to **win** at it."*

– Jack Nicklaus

I've put purpose and motivation together because they are closely linked. Although it's a positive step to create a vision for your future, you need to know *why* it is that you want that life for yourself. Your vision can give you a look at your future life so you can decide if you really want it, and assuming that you do, it will deepen your connection with it. With time being the most valuable commodity, we have to think very carefully about how we will spend it. What it is that truly motivates you to put 100% effort into achieving your vision? How will becoming a champion golfer give your life more meaning?

Your motivation towards your goals will help you give it everything you've got and get you through the inevitable setbacks and struggles ahead.

Answer the questions below to keep peeling back the layers with further "why?" questions until you get to the root of why it is that you are pursuing your vision.

Your long-term success is the accumulation of all the focused effort during each day along the way. What it is that motivates you to put in that effort, will have a big effect on whether you achieve your goals and how happy your pursuit of them will make you. It *has* to be meaningful for you to become successful.

Purpose Exercises:
In your Golf State of Mind notebook, write your answers to the following questions:

> *"Why this vision for my future and not something else?"*
> *"Why will I spend my limited time working hard to pursue this particular endeavor?"*
> *"What is it about this vision/goal that is going to add meaning and purpose to my life?"*
> *"Why is it that I want to compete?"*

Your Player Identity Statement

Results will come and go as there are many things that are out of your control on your journey. Consistency of results isn't possible. However, you can be consistent in the values that you bring to each day and each round. What is at the core of the player that you want to become? This is more important than any score or trophies you might win. Your "Player Values" are the guiding principles for your

Module 1: Self Discovery   **17**

thinking, behaviors and actions. What is it that you stand for and the values that you hold highest? Performance Psychologist, Michael Gervais asks his students to create a "Personal Philosophy Statement" which encapsulates these values. I like to think of it as a "Player Identity Statement" – a declaration of who you will be.

Before each round you will read this statement and make a promise to yourself to uphold it.

Player Identity Exercise:
1. Start by writing a list of all the values that you would like to bring to your practice and play. What do you believe are your keys to high performance? Examples of these are:
   - Discipline
   - Effort
   - Focus
   - Commitment
   - A Positive Attitude
   - Courage
   - Adaptability
   - Humility
   - Competitiveness
   - Gratitude
   - Poise
   - Self-compassion
   - Presence
   - Patience
   - Acceptance
   - Honesty

2. Use these values to create your "Player Identity Statement", which is a promise to yourself for who you will be in your rounds and practice. Here's an example:

"I am Alex and I am fully present to where I am now. I focus on being disciplined to my plan as I know that if I do the right things and believe in myself it will lead me to continued improvement. I strive to be my best self and act with integrity and optimism no matter what obstacles I am faced with or what transpires in a round. I am continually grateful for the opportunity to play this great game."

Mindset

Your mindset:

- Is how you approach a situation or goal
- Is your attitude to challenges and failure
- *Will* affect your long-term success

In this section, I'd like to help you find *your* optimal mindset, or "approach" for learning and competing.

The Optimal Mindset for Learning and Skill Development

In her book: "Mindset: The New Psychology of Success", Professor Carol Dweck of Stanford University tells us of a study she did to determine the effect of praise on the development of young students. 400 students were given a simple, non-verbal test. One half of the group was praised upon their result by saying things such as: *"You are so smart"*.

The second group was praised, not by the result, but by the effort and process they went through to get to the answers, i.e., *"You must have worked very hard to get these answers, well done!"*

Next, the students were given 2 options for a second test. 1. A similar test to the first one, that they should do equally well at, or 2. A more difficult test, but a better opportunity to learn.

The results were compelling. 67% of the group praised for being "smart" went for the first option, as the easier test would guarantee them a similar result.

Surprisingly, 92% of the group praised for effort and process opted for the harder challenge.

What we are shown here is 2 different mindsets for learning. The first group who (because of the way they were praised) became driven by their ego and the feeling of being "smart" again. These students exhibited more of what Professor Dweck calls a "Fixed Mindset". Conversely, the second group, through praise of effort and process that they went through to figure out the solutions, became less motivated by the result they might get and more motivated by the opportunity to learn something new. Professor Dweck says that these students have more of what she calls a "Growth Mindset".

Now imagine that we reinforce this type of thinking over and over again…

I'm sure that you've already concluded that the optimal mindset for learning is the "Growth" or "Mastery" mindset.

Success	Under Achievement
Mastery Mindset	Ego Mindset
Growth Mindset	Fixed Mindset

One of my goals for this training program is to show you ways that you can move yourself away from an Ego Mindset and more towards a Growth Mindset every day. With this mindset you'll realize that your talents and abilities are not fixed, they are limitless. Let's take a deeper look into the traits of both mindsets, so you can learn more about what your current mindset is and start your transformation today.

A Fixed or Ego Mindset

Let's start with the mindset that will hold us back from becoming the best we can be. A person with a Fixed Mindset has the following beliefs:

1. **That you're born with your talents**
   Ability is predetermined and limited by genetics, and we have little power to change it.

2. **The end result and standing against others is the most important thing**

   The result they get on that day defines their current ability level. Because their motivation is more "extrinsic", a performance is either a success or failure based on the result. They miss out on valuable learning opportunities to improve because they are too consumed by the outcome. As shown in Professor Dweck's study, those with a Fixed or Ego Mindset would rather do something easier to get a good result than to do a challenge which they might fail at, even if they will learn more. Without the benefit of being able to look deeper beyond the result and learn, long-term performance is limited.

3. **Scores reflect who you are as a person**

   Because they believe that ability is part of their DNA and who they are, those with a Fixed Mindset struggle to separate themselves from their results. They take bad results personally, and good results can lead to overconfidence. For this reason, they can often fixate on rankings and leaderboards, compare themselves to other players and worry what other people think of them because of their score. Status is important to them and because their view of themselves is tied to results, their confidence can be fragile.

4. **That mistakes show weakness**

   The ego mentality of a Fixed Mindset player makes them vulnerable to (inevitable) mistakes.

The results-based goals and fear of how they will look puts a lot of pressure on every shot. If they make mistakes, they don't cope well and often react emotionally.

Ryan Holiday, author of "The Ego is The Enemy" says: *"Your reputation will take knocks. If it can't handle it, it wasn't that good in the first place."*

5. **That Practice Can Be Wasted Effort**
   Because they believe that their ability is fixed, and they have little control in changing it, Fixed Mindset players aren't as motivated to practice hard. When they do practice, they invariably practice the things they are good at (which satisfies their ego) and avoid those areas that they struggle with.

A Growth or "Mastery" Mindset

"An amateur is defensive. A professional finds learning (and even occasionally being shown up) to be enjoyable. They like being challenged and humbled, and engage in education as an ongoing, endless process."

– Ryan Holiday, The Ego Is The Enemy

Let's take a look at what Professor Carol Dweck tells us about people with a Growth Mindset:

1. **They believe that talent and skills are learned**
   People with a Growth Mindset believe that talent and ability can be improved and learned over

time i.e., you "grow" from your experiences and hard work. Research in the field of neuroscience confirms this is true, and that the brain and neural connections/pathways can change and strengthen, with the right perspective (mindset) and approach to challenges. Daniel Coyle says in his book "The Talent Code": *"Although talent looks and feels predestined, in fact we have a good deal of control over which skills we develop, and we might have more potential that we might ever presume to guess."*

2. **They have a longer-term view of success**
Players with a Growth Mindset have the perspective that every day and every round is a step towards mastering their craft and themselves, whatever the outcome. It doesn't stop when you reach certain goals or have setbacks. The "journey to better" never ends…

3. **They value learning more than the results**
Players with a Growth Mindset have a predisposition towards learning, which increases performance and ability over time. They are curious about every round, no matter what the result. They know that results come and go, but skill development is the key to long-term success.

4. **They are highly motivated**
Players with more of a Growth Mindset are more motivated to work on their game, especially the areas they know they can do better. Because their purpose for playing goes deeper than achieving

results and status, they put in more work, dig deeper, and get more out of themselves. Their goals have more meaning which makes them more motivated to achieve them. Being competitive to a player with a Growth Mindset means using competition to push themselves and learn more about themselves.

5. **They embrace challenges, failures and mistakes**
Also in his book "The Talent Code", Daniel Coyle says *"Struggle is not optional—it's neurologically required: in order to get your skill circuit to fire optimally, you must by definition fire the circuit suboptimally; you must make mistakes and pay attention to those mistakes."*

A person with a Growth Mindset is happy to expose themselves to challenges (and risk failing) as they view them as the best opportunities to develop skills and themselves ("From struggle comes strength"). And there's a further upside to this - because mistakes are more accepted for their learning value, a Growth Mindset person plays with more freedom and less fear, which (ironically) leads to fewer mistakes. Angela Duckworth, author of the book "GRIT", says: *"A Fixed Mindset about ability leads to pessimistic explanations of adversity, and that, in turn, leads to both giving up on challenges and avoiding them in the first place. In contrast, a Growth Mindset leads to optimistic ways of explaining adversity, and that, in turn, leads to perseverance and seeking out new challenges that will ultimately make you even stronger... the secret to outstanding achievement is not talent, but a special blend of passion and persistence."*

6. **They are more in touch with their values and purpose**

    High self-esteem comes from sticking to your values no matter what the outcome. An Ego Mindset player would probably sacrifice their values for a better result. After doing the Player Identity exercise earlier in the module, you should have a better idea of what your values are. Every round is an opportunity to work on becoming the player and person that you want to be, regardless of the result. If you can uphold those values, you will build self-esteem and confidence in yourself.

7. **They are more optimistic**

    Players with a Growth Mindset are generally more positive because of their perspective (i.e., any task is a win-win: you succeed or learn). Because they are convinced that they can keep evolving and benefitting from challenges, they are more optimistic about the future, which improves attitude and performance. People with an optimistic outlook have more good things happen to them!

8. **They welcome feedback and don't compare themselves to others**

    The Growth Mindset golfer welcomes constant feedback directly from their performance and from their coaches. They are honest with themselves about the areas they can get better. They don't need to hear how good they are from others to feel confident or feel the need to compare themselves to others. They are their own measure of success.

9. **They stay humble no matter how successful they become**

   Players with a Growth Mindset deal with winning in a better way than those with an Ego Mindset. Instead of thinking they have it all figured out, they realize that winning is only temporary. They know that if they get complacent (by falling into the ego trap), they will stop growing and their performance will suffer in the long-run. The greats don't take success for granted; they keep working hard on the journey to better.

Steps to Develop more of a Growth Mindset Everyday

1. **Change Your Perspective on Struggle and Failure**

   "I know fear is an obstacle for some people, but it is an illusion to me. Failure always made me try harder next time."

   – **Michael Jordan**

For every player that plays this game, there are more "failures" than there are successes. Most people see failure as a negative word. I'd like you to re-learn it as a positive one. I'm not saying that failing isn't disappointing and painful at times, but it's an essential ingredient in the recipe for success. Failure is the best teacher.

Any situation which challenges you and narrows the margin between success and failure is the optimal learning opportunity. Feeling challenged (both mentally and physically), although uncomfortable at the time, is where deep learning takes place and should be embraced, not shied away from.

When you see failure as an opportunity for growth, the future prospect of it won't worry you as much – you'll be less afraid of it. You'll be able to give more of your mental energy to your process and doing the things that make you your best performing self and you'll play more freely.

2. Keep A "Performance Journal"

Journaling and writing about your experiences is a great way to learn from your experiences and highlight areas that you are growing. After a round or practice session, ask yourself:

- What are the areas of my game that I'm improving?
- What did I learn?
- What will I work on?
- How did I deal with the thoughts and feelings that arose?

3. Measure performance by your Mental Scorecard rather than the result

Results will come and go, but those results shouldn't affect your mindset. With a better mindset every day and every round you will grow over time. Whether you shoot 70 or 80, did you give yourself the best opportunity for success? Ask yourself questions such as: How was my focus, my self talk and my body language? What did I learn and how did I respond to challenges?

As we saw in Professor Dweck's study, simply changing what the students were praised for, changed their mindset. You can do the same with the questions you continually ask yourself and by celebrating the moments where you demonstrated the Growth Mindset.

Your Mental Scorecard is a great tool to keep you more focused on process and learning, instead of ego and results. You can download the scorecard in the next module.

4. Remember that Golf is what you do, *not* who you are

After winning The Players Championship in 2019, Rory McIlroy spoke about how he had made some changes in his mental approach which had helped him take pressure off himself. He said that in the past, he had tied his scores with how he felt about himself as a person which made him push too hard to get results (i.e., he played too much ego golf).

In the off season and early part of 2019, he made an effort to change this mindset and have a new measure of success for his rounds (his process goals), and to do a better job of separating Rory McIlroy "the player", from Rory McIlroy "the person".

Remember that golf is not who you are, it's what you do. With more of a Growth Mindset, you can separate the two, play with more freedom and learn from every round.

A Competitive Mindset

Now that we've identified the overarching mindset that is going to help you continually learn and grow as a player and a person throughout your life, let's identify your best "Competitive Mindset".

What is the ideal mindset for you to perform at your best? By best, I don't mean how do you think and feel when you are playing your best, I mean what is the mindset that will help you get the best out of yourself in every round?

Let's start with a feeling? Are you feeling intense, happy, aggressive, grateful, or excited?

What are the thoughts/words that can create that feeling?

An example is: *"Competition isn't about me against anyone else, it's about trying to be the best version of me. I love a challenge and can deal with any setback. I don't mind being out of my comfort zone - that's where the real "gold" is found, and I can channel my focus and discover more about myself as an athlete. I am optimistic and I know that I can get on a streak any time. I love this game!"*

What are the physical actions that are in line with that mindset?

Do you have a certain posture or walk that goes with that mindset? What physical action could trigger that mindset? Tying your golf shoes or getting the clubs out of the car? Putting on your cap?

Being in a competitive environment is always an opportunity to learn how to find your optimal performance state or tap into what you currently have. Your mindset is your gateway to doing this, so it's key to activate it before you go out to play.

Mindset Exercises:
1. *Describe your mindset for learning, whether it's a Growth or Fixed Mindset*
2. *What is your ideal competitive mindset when you play?*

Assessing Your Mental Game

If you would like to fill out the Golf State of Mind Mental Game Assessment, you can do so by going to this link: https://www.golfstateofmind.com/mental-game-assessment-from-umgts/

Module 2: The Performance Process

In order to become the best player you can be, you'll need to put a plan in place – a set of guidelines and "mini goals" so that you get the best out of yourself daily and in your rounds. Success with this plan is not based on score or results, but by completion of certain tasks and how much effort you give to them. These tasks will keep you focused on what's most important for growth and higher levels of performance.

This series of tasks and intentions to get the best out of yourself is called your "Performance Process". Although we're covering this early in the program, as you go through the modules and discover more about yourself and the tools you have available to you, you can refine and add to it. To help you understand the difference between "process" and "outcome", let's do an exercise:

1. *Get a sheet of paper and divide it into 2 columns. In the first column, write down your goals for a round of golf. Move to step 2 once you have done this*
2. *In the second column, next to those goals, write down (with a "Yes" or "No"), whether you have 100% control over achieving that goal or not*

Outcome Goals

If you did the exercise above, I'm sure that at least some of the things that you put into your goals column would have been desired outcomes, such as your score, fairways and greens hit, and number of putts. Or perhaps you put some goals down in terms of avoiding undesirable outcomes such as "No 3 Putts". Either way, these are all "Outcome Goals". If you consider whether these are 100% within your control or not, you will have a "No" for them in the 2nd column.

The negative effects of outcome goals
It goes without saying that everyone that plays golf would like good outcomes - to shoot a low score, hit good shots and play well. That is obviously preferable to playing poorly. However, when you are performing any action and you are concerned as to what the outcome of that action will be, it can make achieving it more difficult.

A simple illustration of this is a golfer telling me that they can play great on the range, but on the course they are unable to play to the same level. Clearly their focus shifts and their internal state changes when there is a consequence to their shots, and they are accountable for how many of them they play.

In golf, there are many variables and events that are uncertain, such as:

- The outcome of each shot
- Your lie on the fairway, in the rough or in a bunker

- The bounce the ball takes
- How your playing partners play, their personalities and their playing speed
- The weather
- Where you finish in the tournament
- What other people might think about you and your game

If we allow such things to take our attention away from the tasks we need to complete to hit the next shot well, it will negatively impact performance.

Why can outcome focus work against you?

1. It takes you out of the present moment - the mind isn't quiet and fully focused on what you need to do now
2. The fear of not meeting your outcome goals for a shot or round can create performance anxiety and increase nerves and tension in the body
3. It can cause you to get emotional as you judge the outcome of each shot as to whether it helps or hurts you achieving your outcome goals
4. It can affect your motivation and effort i.e., if you predict you will reach your outcome goal you put in effort but if you predict you won't, it can cause you to lower effort or give up
5. It can cause you to miss out on appreciating the experience of playing golf – there is so much

more to it than your score, but this is missed when success is measured by outcome

Let's take a look at a couple of examples:

Example 1:
Let's say you've got the goal of shooting under a certain score and avoiding 3-putts in a round. Because a good score is at the forefront of your mind, you want to get off to a good start. But because of the self-imposed pressure, you double bogey the first hole and have a 3 putt (which is possible for the best players in the world). With your chances of achieving your outcome goals taking a big hit on the first hole, you will have to deal with the negative emotions and added pressure to turn it around. It can also cause you to play more aggressively to get those shots back, potentially leading to more big numbers.

Example 2:
Let's say you've had your best front nine ever. Perhaps you didn't know what your score was until you checked it at the half-way point, but now you know you're playing as good as you can play. Because of this, your mind shifts from the present to the future and the desired outcome of shooting your best score or the undesirable outcome of not taking advantage of such a good opportunity. The combination of excitement and fear from allowing your attention to focus on these possibilities will probably make you feel nervous and anxious, and most likely cause you to lose focus on your shots and tense up.

This is why so many players fall back into their comfort zone when they're playing well or in contention in a tournament.

Whether it's focusing on achieving positive outcomes or avoiding negative outcomes, focus on outcome goals should generally be avoided before and during your rounds. I'm not saying that this will be easy or black and white just because you choose it. Thoughts about score can and will pop into your mind, but with increased awareness and improved focus, you will be able to shift your attention away from them and back to what you need to do in the present moment.

The positive effects of outcome goals
Some players benefit from outcome goals. As long as you are not thinking about outcome goals as you play a shot, they can raise intensity and focus. This is something for you to explore and possibly use to control your internal state and push you into "flow state".

Try playing 6 x 3-hole matches against old man par. 6 matches gives you 6 times to reset during the round and each time you are using the outcome goal of trying to beat par (or whatever your par is).

I've heard many players tell me they can raise their performance by telling themselves: *"Let's make some birdies"* or *"I can birdie this hole"*, the prospect of that (outcome) excites them and increases their focus and energy.

In the previous module, we created your "vision" for your game, which involves visualizing the future outcome of your efforts today. This vision is a form of an outcome goal which shows you what you want to create for yourself in the future (and why) which can increase motivation and effort today.

However, once we set an outcome goal, we have to let go of it and focus solely on the plan to take us there.

Defining "Process"

Unlike outcome, which is uncertain and focusing on it can have negative effects, a process is a series of intentions and actions that we *know* will increase our chances of success. If you can execute your process, *you are doing your best*.

Your Process is:
- Your plan for improving your game
- Focal cues for your shot routines
- A set of guidelines to help you control your internal state during rounds

Why Process Focus Improves Performance

The Brain Prefers Certainty

The human brain prefers security and certainty rather than uncertainty. Certainty initiates a reward response, whereas uncertainty initiates the fight or flight response. When your focus is on aspects of your performance which are uncertain, your sympathetic nervous system prepares your body and mind to deal with the unknowns or possible threats. We know this as nerves, performance anxiety or "the fight or flight response". I'm not saying that nerves and raised intensity can't help performance or getting into "flow", but too much outcome focus can take a player beyond that level and performance will suffer. Your process helps you stay poised, present and confident.

Your Process is Present
Whenever we can bring our full attention to what we are doing now, and *not* think about how the outcome of it will affect us in the future, we are going to perform better.

The best place for your mind in any round is in the present moment. The present is where your mind is calm and focused on what you are doing now.

When the mind goes into predicting mode or you are thinking about what's going to happen next, you are in the future. When you are unable to move on from the last bad shot or 3-putt, you are in the past. Neither of these "time zones" are helpful to you on the golf course.

Your process reminds you exactly what you should be focusing on at this very moment, now, so you get deep into the task at hand.

Your Process is what you do when you perform your best
If you know what gets you into the best mental and physical state to play well, then it makes sense for you

to focus on doing those things. This will require self-discovery, reflection and thought which I will prompt throughout this program. In time, you'll understand more about what triggers your "Flow State".

Your Process is Emotionally Neutral
With a measure of success that is 100% within your control and certain, it's easier to stay emotionally neutral and not react, i.e., if you executed your shot routine and that was the goal of the shot, it's easier to accept the outcome whatever it was. Emotions can draw energy and focus away from the task at hand (the shot).

Your Process Distracts the Ego
The ego mind can easily sabotage our efforts by outcome thinking and predicting what will happen next. We can become distracted from the present and what is most important for us to perform well. The ego mind needs to be brought back into the present and re-focused on "the process".

Your Process is your Plan
Your process is your plan for a round or practice session. Before you go out to play or practice, your process should be decided upon. I also like to think of it as a series of "internal goals" - those things that you can do that you know will positively influence your performance. This turns something complex (shooting a good score), into simple executable steps. With repetition, it becomes more automatic and requires less thinking, so you free

up mental energy for engaging your senses fully in each shot.

This is why I created my "Mental Scorecard" to help players track process, stay accountable and train focus with each round.

If you can set process goals for your rounds, you'll immediately lower distraction and performance anxiety and increase your confidence and chances of playing well.

So what does a "process" look like? To start building your process, let's think about what needs to go into each phase of a performance.

The Phases of Performance

Pre Round
What will you do before your rounds to make you feel confident, prepared, and activate your competitive mindset?

Pre Shot
What are the best things for you to focus on as you prepare for a shot? What is the mental and physical process? Is it breathing, visualization or self talk?

During the Shot
Where is your focus during your swing? Do you have a technical cue?

Post Shot
How will you respond to the outcome of all your shots?

In between Shots
What will you focus on in between shots to keep yourself present and conserving mental energy?

Post Round
How will you review your rounds and measure your success?

Practice Time
What are the performance goals you are working towards? What do you need to *do* to work towards those goals?

Print and fill out the "Process Goals Sheet" which you can find on this page along with all the other program resources: https://golfstateofmind.com/module-resources-email/

This will be your first pass at your "Performance Process" – you will add to it or refine it as we go through the program.

The Mental Scorecard

The goal of the Mental Scorecard is to keep you focused on your values and your "Process Goals" during your rounds and help you define success as getting the best out of yourself in every moment, no matter what game you have that day. I have two versions of the scorecard.

The Hole by Hole Mental Scorecard
The first is a simpler version that has you score your mental game or process by hole. For each round, you

would decide on 4 process goals to score yourself by, such as:

- Picking a clear target and visualizing each shot
- Choosing to respond well and take a positive from each shot
- A deep breath before walking into the ball
- Having a good tempo
- Being present and grateful in between shots
- Having confident body language

Modules 3 and 4 will help you decide upon the best process goals for you. If you achieve all 4 of your process goals for that hole, you will give yourself 4 points in the box on the scorecard, so you will have a total score out of 72. You can download this template on the resources page: https://golfstateofmind.com/module-resources-email/

Alternatively, if you want to simplify it even further, you can give yourself a checkmark for each hole that you achieved *all* your Process Goals (so a maximum score of 18 per round).

The Shot Routine Mental Scorecard
The other version of the Mental Scorecard focuses solely on the Shot Routine.

For each of the 3 types of shot (Full Shot, Short Game and Putting), you will select 4 process goals.

If you achieve *all* 4 process goals during a single shot, you get one point which you would add in the box for that hole on the scorecard. E.g., if you had a 5 on a hole, but you went through your 4 process goals for 3 of them, you would have 3 points for that hole. The scoring system for each shot is "binary", you either get a 1 or 0. 1 would be for completing all 4 of your process goals.

Your total process score will show you how many shots you were able to execute while going through your intended shot routine. You can then calculate the percentage of shots that you achieved your process out of your total actual score. E.g., 65 process points out of a total actual score of 75 would be 65/75 x 100 = 87%.

The template for this version is also available on the resources page.

Your process goals don't have to be set in stone but stick to them for at least a few rounds, before making changes to them. You can review and refine them during the post round review.

Being Present and Directing Attention

> *"I just stay in the moment. I never think one hole ahead. I'm not thinking about tomorrow. I'm not thinking about the next shot. I'm just thinking about what I need to do right now. It's very simple."*
> **– Brooks Koepka**

Being "in the present" and "in the process" go hand in hand. Whether you are practicing or playing, if you intend to do it as best you can, you'll need to be present and direct your focus to the task at hand.

Unfortunately, most of us spend time switching between time zones (the past, present and future), or we are distracted in and out of tasks meaning we need to constantly re-focus. In golf, our mistakes or lost opportunities can cause us to think about the past, whereas excitement or fear can shift focus to the future. Being in either the past or future during our rounds is not conducive to high performance – we lose focus on the process, and whatever we place our attention on (external outcomes or internal thoughts) can change the way we feel.

The optimal place for high performance and learning, is the present moment. In fact, the definition of "The Zone" or "Flow State" - which you probably know as the state of mind where peak performance happens - is being completely *immersed* in an activity. There's no daydreaming or judgment, there is *only* what we are doing now.

Without a clear process or plan, it's harder to stay present as you won't have the focal cues necessary to keep your attention on what is most productive for you in the present, i.e., if you know your process you already know what to bring your attention to NOW. This could be as simple as focusing on your breathing in between shots.

In order to keep our attention on what's most important (or away from what isn't), we need to develop awareness of our attention. If we are unaware of where our minds are, our mood can be controlled by whatever thoughts pop into our heads, or whatever happens in the round. We need to be able to notice thoughts, but (through an awareness practice), let them pass if they are unhelpful. I recommend starting an awareness practice, such as mindfulness meditation which I'll cover in module 4.

Process Goal Exercises:
1. *Before your next round, print out the Process Goals sheet and write in your Player Identity Statement, Routines and Reminders*
2. *Print out a version of the Mental Scorecard, enter your process goals and track them during your next round*
3. *Are there any outcome goals that could be helpful to you? Is any type of score focus necessary to raise your focus and intensity level?*

Module 3: The Shot Routine

The shot routine plays a large part in how well you access your best skills and execute the shot in front of you.

In this module, I'll give you a plan for finding your best Shot Routine, based on your learning style, what you do when you're playing your best shots, and what your tendencies are under pressure. The steps of your Shot Routine should become mini goals and will be a key performance indicator for your rounds.

The Phases of The Shot Routine

Over the time that I've worked with hundreds of players on the mental side of the game, I can safely say that there is no one shot routine that works best for every player. What you decide to focus on during your shot routine will require experimentation and self-discovery to figure out. The purpose of any "routine" is that it becomes habitual. The more you follow the steps of your shot routine, the more automatic it will become in the pressure moments. This routine should be practiced as much as possible, not just when you are on the course. You should be training your attention as much as you train your golf swing.

Let's start with the fundamentals of the shot routine that will be the same for every player.

1. **Switching On Your "Golf Brain"**
   With such a large part of a round of golf spent not playing, an important skill is to be able to switch on and switch off your golf brain

2. **Analytical/Planning Phase (Pre Shot Routine)**
   This part of the Pre Shot Routine is about picking the best shot to hit, considering the unique challenge in front of you

3. **Rehearsal/Creative Phase (Pre Shot Routine)**
   Once you've decided on the best shot to hit, you'll need to turn your intention into sensations. What will the shot look, feel and sound like?

4. **Engagement/Athletic Phase (Pre Shot Routine)**
   How will you walk into the ball and what will you focus on before starting your swing to ensure that you are athletic

5. **The Shot**
   Where will your focus be during your swing?

6. **Acceptance Phase (Post Shot Routine)**
   How will you accept and process the outcome of the shot, so you can return to the present as quickly as possible?

Now let's build *your* Pre Shot Routine.

Module 3: The Shot Routine

The Pre Shot Pyramid

Engagement Phase
Full commitment
Holding onto sensation from rehearsal phase
Full engagement with target
Quiet mind
External focus

Rehearsal Phase
Rehearse shot focusing on the sensations which you've determined connect you best with a shot (visual, feel or sound)

Thinking Phase
What is the best target and shot given the unique sitation of what's around the target, the lie, wind, relationship of ball to stance etc.?

The Goals Of The Pre Shot Routine

What is the purpose of The Pre Shot Routine?

- To "switch on" your focus and get you prepared for the shot as best you can
- To ensure that you pay attention to all the available information to select the optimal strategy and shot
- To make sure you approach each shot with the same mindset
- To focus *only* on what you can control and tune out the noise (negative thoughts) that will try to

- pull you away the present moment and what's most important
- To increase commitment and connect you with the sensations (visual, feel, sound) of the shot
- To make every shot feel the same

Step 1: Switching on your "Golf Brain"

Your "golf brain" only needs to be fully engaged for the time from when you arrive at your ball (or tee it up), to shortly after you've finished your shot. The rest of the time, you'll be doing your best to relax and stay present.

The better your relaxation in between shots, the better your concentration during shots. For this reason, every shot should have a beginning and an end.

When the shot begins, you *switch on* your golf brain and when it's over, you *switch off* your golf brain.

One way to do this is using some sort of a signal or a "trigger" at the beginning of your Pre Shot Routine and at the end of the post shot routine. Let's start with the "Switch on" trigger.

If you watch the Pre Shot Routines of the world's best players you'll notice they might do certain things "routinely" as they prepare to play their shot, such as tapping the ground with their club, adjusting their cap or their shirt. It's likely these are triggers to bring them into the here and now and switch on their golf brain.

Here are some examples of Pre Shot Triggers:
- A deep breath
- A verbal cue or trigger word, like "let's go!"

- Putting on your glove
- Taking off your sunglasses
- Looking at your Mental Scorecard
- A sound like snapping the Velcro on your glove
- Taking a sip from your water bottle
- A smile or adjusting your posture

Triggers become more powerful with practice, so make sure you spend some time using them during practice, not just when you are playing competitively.

Step 2: The Planning Phase

Once you are focused, it's time to plan your strategy, pick your target and choose the type of shot and club to play.

This type of "cognitive" thinking is done by the part of the brain called the Prefrontal Cortex. This same part of the brain is NOT particularly good at athletic movement, which is why it's important to do your thinking first, so you're fully committed to the shot, and you can be athletic over the ball and during the swing.

Picking the best target and shot for a given situation is also known as "GOLF I.Q." A player with a high Golf I.Q. will start putting their course strategy together before the round, so they have information to hand such as:

- Carry distances for tee shots and approaches
- The width of the fairways at different distances off the tee
- The best angles to hit their approach shots from

- The areas they can miss off the tee and from approaches
- The green contours so they have more uphill chips and putts than downhill

We'll talk more about Planning for a round in Module 5. During the Planning Phase of the Pre Shot Routine, you'll need to ask yourself the following questions. This might sound like a lot at first, but with practice and preparation, it will take no more than 1-2 minutes to pick the right shot.

"What is my strategy? What is Possible and What is Probable?"
For every shot, there are several options for shots that you could play. The first step is to try to figure out the probability of you executing each option, so you find a balance of risk and reward that you feel comfortable with. Doing this well means that you will minimize mistakes and maximize opportunities to score.

Let's start with what you think the perfect shot is (what is possible) and then work towards the best shot for you to hit, based on your confidence level and probability of executing it. You will need to figure out the details of each option, such as the distance to carry, the width of the landing areas, your lie, elevation changes between you and the target, etc.

Factoring in Your "Dispersion"
If you were to see a map of your last 100 7 irons you hit on the course, there would be a spray or "dispersion" of

Module 3: The Shot Routine   51

the shots in relation to the target. Even the best players in the world have a dispersion to their shots and know that in any round that it's possible that they can miss several fairways and greens (Tour player average is 60-70% of fairways and greens hit).

As Ben Hogan once said: *"This is a game of misses. The guy who misses the best is going to win."*

Most launch monitors can show you what your dispersion is for each club, which can be very helpful for your course strategy. This data is even more accurate if it's your actual shots on the course, which you can obtain using some GPS shot tracking devices E.g., You would know that when you hit 100 shots with your 7 iron, the dispersion of the balls is 50 yards from left to right (meaning that your worst shots could be 25 yards either side of your intended target). Tour player average dispersion with a 7 iron is approximately 40 yards (or 20 yards left or right of the target).

Let's see how this could be useful in the following scenario: You have a 7 iron approach shot. There is water 10 yards to the right of the green and the pin is 5 yards from the right edge of the green It's a big green that is 30 yards wide with little trouble to the left (for simplicity we'll assume that the pin is center-right, so there's no better miss long or short). If you know that your dispersion from your intended target is 20 yards either way, then going at the pin brings the water into play and a possibly tough chip from being short-sided. Assuming no wind, the optimal target here is the left center of the green (20 yards from the right edge of the green), allowing for the possible 20-yard dispersion right or left. Even a right miss to this target is a good outcome as you get close to the pin, but this strategy reduces the possibility of the shot into the water, or "a big number" to almost zero.

In the example above, the area left of the green is called "the good miss" and missing to the right of the green would clearly be "the bad miss". I.e., Even if you have a very long putt or chip from missing the green left, it's still better than the penalty shot and drop that you would face from hitting the water.

Knowing *where* you can miss your target to avoid the big numbers and still get up and down, is not a negative thought, but a smart one. I hear many Tour players talk about adopting a "conservative-aggressive strategy". What this means, is that they know where they can miss and still give themselves a chance of scoring. Once they establish this, they can be free to swing more aggressively to that target, knowing they have the buffer for the inevitable dispersion in their shots.

How confident do I feel?
Your confidence at the time is a factor in shot selection. On some days you just feel more confident in your game, and during those rounds (where you have your "A game"), you will have more "green light" shots, where you can be a little more aggressive and take on more risk. However, during most rounds, you won't have your A game or feel good about your swing. Jack Nicklaus said that he only felt good about his swing about 20% of the

time. On the days when you have your B, C, or D game, you'll need to pick more conservative targets and a more controllable shot, so you feel comfortable over the ball. Those are not the days to try to force a good score or make up strokes. Picking higher risk shots means that you'll feel more stressed over the ball which can lead to more execution mistakes. If you're over a shot and you feel comfortable with your shot selection, your mind will be quieter and your swing more relaxed, leading to better shots. After a few safer shots, it's possible that you can start playing better and take on a little more risk.

Know The Course
Good golf courses are designed to trick players by making them think there is less room off the tee and from approaches than there actually is. Looking at the aerial views using your yardage book (or Google Earth before the round) will tell you how much room you have, so you can pick better lines. Walking the course backwards is another way to see what is real and not what the course designer wants you to think from the tee or your approach shots to the green.

By the end of the Planning Phase, you should feel like you have a shot that you could execute *at least* 75% of the time and be 100% committed to it.

Other course strategy questions:
- *How hard/soft is the green or fairway?*
- *Which side of the fairway is best to get a good angle to the green with my approach?*

- *What is the optimal trajectory?*
- *Will I have an uphill putt or downhill putt if I hit my target on the green?*
- *Will the next shot be one of my strengths?*
- *Is there an elevation change between me and my target?*
- *How far is it to "cover" a carry and how far is it to the end of my target area?*

Target Orientation
It goes without saying that you need a target for your shot, but one player's target could look differently to another player. You might have heard the phrase *"aim small miss small"*, but small targets don't work for all players. Some players can feel restricted and tighten up with a smaller target compared to a wider target area (like "goalposts") to hit into.

Some players will have a small starting target and small finishing target, whereas other players could have a small starting target and wider landing area. Some players have their targets on the horizon and others have them at ground level. There are several options for target orientation, so you will need to practice and find out what works best for you. I have some drills in the practice book that you can use to work on this.

Step 3: The Rehearsal Phase

The next step of your Shot Routine is the Rehearsal Phase. The purpose of this phase is to prime your body

Module 3: The Shot Routine

and mind to play the shot that you've decided upon in the Planning Phase. Your swing will benefit from your brain connecting with a sensory representation of the shot, so it knows which neural pathways and muscles to activate during the swing. Here are some ways you can rehearse a shot before you play it. Experiment with them and find out *your* best way for you to rehearse a shot.

Visual Rehearsal or "Visualization"

> *"I never hit a shot, not even in practice, without having a very sharp, in focus picture of it in my head. It's like a color movie. First, I see the ball where I want it to finish, nice and white and sitting up high on bright green grass. Then the scene quickly changes, and I see the ball going there: its path, trajectory and shape, even its behavior on landing. Then there is a sort of fade out and the next scene shows me making the kind of swing that will turn the previous images into reality."*
> **- Jack Nicklaus**

Why does visualization work?
Once you've figured out your strategy, target and type of shot you are going to hit, you will benefit from anticipating what it will look like. Many players (like the great Jack Nicklaus) find that creating a visual image of the shot in their "mind's eye" gives them a better chance of hitting it.

I should add here that from my experience, some players find visualization in the way Jack described easier than others, and it doesn't mean that if you can't visualize a shot in this way that you can't become as good as someone who can. There are several ways to "visualize" a shot that your body can subconsciously react to, and you need to experiment and find what works best for you.

The reason that visualization works (or any type of "rehearsal" for that matter) is because it sends messages to the movement centers of your brain which organize your movement during the swing or putting stroke.

Every shot you hit leaves an internal representation (visual, feel, sound, etc.) in your brain. The more sensory feedback you get from your shots, the better you get at noticing and storing what you have experienced. This is another reason why the Post Shot Routine is important – to store the look, feel and sound of your good shots. E.g., a 5 yard fade into the green will have a distinct look, feel and sound to you. This is why random practice is effective, as you get to experience the sensations of a variety of different shots.

When you visualize a 5 yard fade, your brain can subconsciously recall a feel associated with it, which it can turn into a movement pattern. This doesn't require you to consciously think about the swing you need to hit a 5 yard fade, it's just there, associated with that specific shot. Another example of this is how a Tour pro is able to hit an exact yardage for a wedge shot without consciously doing anything different with their swing. By simply thinking of the yardage, e.g., "73 yards" they subconsciously find the swing that hit the ball that far.

Module 3: The Shot Routine   57

To illustrate the power of visualization, have you ever noticed that when you're faced with a tough shot out of trouble, you're often able to pull it off, whereas you can sometimes miss a relatively easy shot into the green from the fairway? One possible reason for this, is because you have a much clearer intention (or visualization) and higher level of focus for the more challenging shot. By simply asking yourself: *"What am I trying to achieve here?",* you can often produce the swing to do it. During a more challenging shot, the swing is more "subconscious" and fluid because more of your focus and mental energy is directed towards the intention for it.

Let's take a look at a couple of case studies that show scientific proof of the positive effects of visualization.

Case Study 1: How Visualization Improves Putting
In a study at the Olympic Training Center in Colorado, they tested the effect of visualization on a group of 30 golfers.

The group was randomly divided into 3 sub-groups of 10 players, to conduct a test on the effect of visualization on putting.

To begin, each group did a series of putting drills using their normal putting routine.

Next, the first group was asked to perform the same drills as before, but this time thinking *only* about their stroke. The second group was asked to do detailed visualization of the line and speed of the putt and where on the hole the ball would enter. The third group was asked to visualize the ball finishing short of the hole

on each putt. After a week of doing these same putting drills each day, they were asked to do them again using their normal putting routine. The results compared to their first attempt were as follows:
- The group that just practiced the stroke improved by 11%
- The group that visualized each putt following its line to the hole and going in, improved by 30%
- The group that visualized the ball finishing short, worsened by 21%!!!

Case study 2: The Effect of Visualization on Body Movement

In 1977, Psychologist Dr. Richard Suinn did a study to test the hypothesis that by visualizing a downhill ski race, skiers would activate the same muscles they would if they were actually skiing. If this was true, then visualization could be used as an effective way to train. The skiers had electrodes attached to their bodies (to detect muscle activity) and, with their eyes closed, Dr. Suinn had them imagine skiing down a specific downhill ski run. The hypothesis was proven to be true, with each turn and mogul that they pictured in their minds, the same muscle patterns were fired as would have been on the real ski run.

This is the same thing that happens with the visualization of a golf shot. If you were to close your eyes (like Jason Day does his Pre Shot Routine), and visualize yourself hitting a specific shot, your stored memories of the sensations of that shot would activate the muscles required to hit it. Another way to think about this is each shot having a specific code, and visualization sends that code to your brain to activate a unique sequence of muscle movements. Visualizing the shot you want to hit isn't going to guarantee you hit it every time, but it's proven to get better results than not doing it.

Many other studies prove that imagined actions have a similar "internal representation" (mental and physiological) as actual, real experiences. In other words, visualization is proven to improve performance and increase skill acquisition in practice.

Studies show that visualization:

1. Gives you a clear intention for what you are about to do which increases commitment and reduces doubt
2. Primes your mind and body to anticipate what will happen during the shot
3. Keeps focus more external, so you are less mechanical and more athletic
4. Increases confidence

What type of visualization is best for you?
We all see the world in slightly different ways. We communicate and learn in different ways. This is why I evaluate a new student with my mental game assessment and have them experiment in practice, so we can develop the optimal process for that individual player. Let's take a look at some of the different ways that you can "visualize", so you can begin experimenting.

Outcome Visualization

Outcome visualization is where you create a visual representation of how the ball will move from where it is now, to its final resting point.

There are several ways that you can do this. I should add here that the way you visualize a shot could be different for full shots, short game shots and putts. E.g., you might only imagine the flight or path of the ball for short game shots and putts, whereas your longer shots are more about static targets than the shape of the ball flight. Here are some ways to visualize the outcome of your shots:

- Imagine a color or black and white movie of the ball flight
- Imagine a colored line to represent the ball-flight, like the Shot Tracer technology used on TV coverage. Experiment with different thicknesses and colors for the line
- Is the image of the shot moving or a static picture?
- Visualize the start of the shot, the apex or the ball coming down to the target. Experiment with each of the 3 parts
- What is the shape and trajectory of the ball flight? Fade, draw or straight? Low, medium or high?
- Some players see an imaginary window in front of them to hit the ball through (for a tee or approach shot)

Process Visualization

Another type of visualization is to visualize the swing you will make to create the shot. It could be the club coming into the ball, what your finish will look like, or seeing yourself make the swing as if you are watching yourself on TV. This type of visualization is called "process visualization", or external perspective. My experience suggests that this works best alongside outcome visualization, rather than on its own.

Experiment with these different types of visualization during your next practice session and write down your observations in your practice journal.

Physical Rehearsal

Almost every player takes at least one "practice swing" to physically rehearse the shot. However, there should be a clear intention and purpose for these rehearsal swings. The ultimate goal of a physical rehearsal is to prime your athletic mind and give yourself an improved chance of physically executing the shot. From my experience, here are the different ways you can physically rehearse a shot.

Technical Rehearsal

There are plenty of players who feel more confident about their swing if they do a technical rehearsal. A technical rehearsal can be something you are working on in your swing – a position you want to get into – or an adjustment to your swing based on your miss on that day. Either way, the rehearsal phase is the time to do this, not during the shot.

Be careful that you don't get overly technical and become disconnected from your intention. If you do prefer a technical rehearsal, follow it up with at least one non-technical rehearsal swing where you are focusing on the sensations of the swing for the shot you are about to hit.

Feeling the Shot
If you are about to play a fade shot, feel a fade swing. If it's a low shot, feel a low shot in your rehearsal swings. Your subconscious mind can remember that feeling and it's more likely to reproduce it during your actual swing (so you don't have to consciously think about it).

Tiger Woods says that after he decides on the shot he's going to play, he feels the shot with his hands during his rehearsal swings and he can still feel that sensation when he's over the ball getting ready to play his shot.

Experiment anticipating what impact will feel like for the shot you are about to hit. By creating a feel for path, face angle, low point and angle of attack at impact, it can help you create a swing to achieve it when the club strikes the ball.

Auditory (Sound) Rehearsal

If you're more auditory, you can try imagining the rhythm and tempo of the shot. Tempo is one aspect of the golf swing that can change (especially under pressure) and give you different outcomes. For that reason, it's a good idea to rehearse it before you play your shots.

How long will the back-swing and downswing take and what is the tempo? What is the sound of impact? Can you hear the woosh of a pure strike before you hit it? Fred Couples says his pre shot rehearsal is predominantly about rhythm and tempo.

Verbal Rehearsal

If you're more verbal, you will benefit from verbally describing certain aspects of the shot or your swing to yourself. Some players tell me that when they have a caddie it increases their commitment to their shots and improves their execution. My response to these players is to always be your own "Inner Caddie" who is there before you hit *every* shot. Tell him/her what you intend to do with your swing and the shot.

As you can now see, there are many ways to prime your mind to hit a shot and increase your success. Experiment with these in practice and write your observations down in your practice journal.

Rehearsal Exercises:
What does your Target look like for Tee shots, Approaches, Short Game and Putting?
What is the best way for you to mentally and physically rehearse your shots?

Step 4: Set Up and Alignment

Alignment is the fundamental that requires the most maintenance and you should practice it regularly. This is why you see the best players in the world with their alignment sticks down while practicing on the driving range. Even small changes in alignment and ball position can cause big changes in dispersion. I like to use the same alignment technique as Justin Rose. The basic concept is that it's a lot easier to align properly to something that's close to you, than it is to something far away in the distance. For this reason, you'll need to find an intermediary target to align to, that's closer to the ball. To find this target, you'll need to be looking down the ball-to-target line, rather than from over the ball.

If you're shaping a shot, you'll be aligning to the line you intend the ball to start on. For a straight shot, you'll be aiming directly at your target.

To use this alignment technique, you'll need to know which eye is your "dominant" eye. If you don't know this, use this exercise:

1. Hold your hands out at arm's length and, with both eyes open, make a circle with your fingers and thumbs around a ball like in this photo:

Module 3: The Shot Routine 65

2. Now close one eye, while keeping the other open and do the opposite open/close combination. One of your eyes will keep the ball in the middle of the circle and the other will move it towards the edge of the circle. The eye that keeps the ball more in the middle is your dominant eye

How to find your "spot"
1. With your non-dominant eye closed and your dominant eye open, hold up the shaft of the club as in this photo:

2. Use the shaft of the club to form a line between the middle of the ball and the target
3. Find a "spot" that's 6 inches in front of the ball along the shaft of the club. This could be a piece of grass or anything that stands out to you.

When you get over the ball, imagine a line that extends from the ball through this spot and set your clubface square to it, so the leading edge is pointing directly at it. Set your body in position in relation to this line. Most players set their body up square (or parallel) to the ball-to-target line, but some players set up a little closed or open to the ball-to-target line. Whatever you do, make it intentional and fit the shot you are about to hit

Feel Comfortable, Centered, and Balanced in your Set Up
Once you are in position, do a quick check. Do you feel set up correctly for the shot you are about to hit? Does the ball position match the intention for the shot? Are you feeling centered and balanced?

Step 5: The Athletic Phase

The Athletic Phase is the time from when you start your walk into the ball to when you start your back-swing. During this time, it's imperative that you stay committed to your intention and be "athletic", rather than being in your head, or thinking. This is where you make the transition from conscious, to subconscious. Like with every part of the performance process, this is something that you need to have a plan for and practice.

The "Athletic Mind"

Too many players have good technical skills, but they can't perform well because they get in their own way in the critical moments. If you're over the ball and telling yourself what you *don't* want to do or giving yourself a lesson, your athletic movement will be restricted.

Consider other sports such as soccer, basketball, and tennis, where during most of the game, the ball is moving. In these games, there's little time to think about what you are going to do, you just react to what is happening. Your movement is subconscious, i.e., done without thinking. This improves execution by allowing the movement to be more fluid, not restricted by thinking about doing it correctly or doubts about the outcome. During *athletic* movement, the thinking mind is quiet - you're simply trusting your instincts and what your senses are telling you.

Unlike other sports, in golf the ball is stationary before you start your swing, which gives you plenty of time to think. But to be more successful at it, you will need to learn how to turn off thinking (during this phase the shot routine) and focus on something that is going to connect the movement centers in your brain with your intention for the shot. By doing this, you'll have your "Athletic Mind" fully engaged and increase your chances of success. In this section we're going to look at some effective ways that you can do it.

The Flow State
The studies that have been done on the minds of the top athletes during performance, show that certain changes occur in the brain. During the "Flow" state, the athlete is just doing and not thinking, brain wave frequencies change from high frequency "beta" waves

to lower frequency "alpha" waves. When these brain waves are being transmitted, the player is present, alert, aware and their movement is athletic and uninhibited. The optimal state of mind for performing any athletic movement is where there is zero interference from the thinking or analytical brain, instead there is only doing.

Someone who has spent years studying the anatomy of Flow States is Steven Kotler of Flow Research Collective. In his many books on the subject, Kotler highlights the research which shows that the top athletes have trained their brains to make the stages of brain function during a performance (problem solving, pre-action, action, and post-action evaluation) happen very quickly and require less brain power, or less "thinking".

If this process is broken down and practiced, it can happen at greater speeds during performance. This is something I work on with students during "Performance Practice" where they are put under pressure to test their ability to execute the process. Kotler talks about how the pioneer of "Flow State" research (and the person to coin the term "Flow"), Mihály Csíkszentmihályi (pronounced "Me-High Chick-Sent-Me-High"), shows that when people are in flow, there is less use of the thinking part of the brain called the Prefrontal Cortex. They are not inhibited by the desire to control the action and the outcome. They see what they need to do using only their implicit system (or subconscious mind).

In martial arts, they call this state "Mushin" or "emptiness of mind" where the fighter stops thinking and is completely in the present with heightened sensory awareness. This reduces the fear caused from over thinking and gives them more time to anticipate their opponent's moves.

In the same way, batters in baseball who describe being in Flow say that they see a pitch (which often comes at 90mph) happening in slow motion, giving them plenty of time to hit it.

Unfortunately, we can't *choose* to get into Flow, but there are certain triggers that make it more likely to occur.

Discovering your "Flow Triggers" and practicing focusing your attention on these things during your Pre Shot Routine, will increase the number of times you experience it and improve your performance.

Being more present and being able to choose what you pay attention to is a skill and something we will talk more about later. Here are some suggestions for what to focus on in The Athletic Phase of the Pre Shot Routine. Experiment with them and find out which Flow Triggers work best for you.

Breathe!

A deep breath before you start your walk into the ball is a good way to pause, center yourself in the present moment and get oxygen into your body.

Your Walk into the Ball

"If you look as if you are in control, you probably are".
— **Dr. Dave Alred**

Few players think about the importance of their walk into the ball. Your body language and cadence of your walk will be a factor in how you feel when you're over the ball. Watch any Tour player and you'll see that they look as if they are in control as they walk into the ball.

Good posture, body language and facial expressions are proven to trigger "feel-good" chemicals. How do you want to feel as you walk into the ball? Confident? Excited? Powerful? Create that feeling with your body language and facial expressions. If you want to feel happy, try smiling as you walk in. You can make your walk to the ball even more intentional by approaching the ball from the same angle and taking the same number of steps into your set-up position.

Make it Quick and Reactive

Once you get over the ball, it's time to be "athletic", not static.

Studies done on the relationship between process and performance show that the consistency of the Pre Shot Routine and time spent over the ball are major factors in the player's performance.

One such study, done by Dr. Mark Bridges at the University of Birmingham in England, concluded that:

1. Spending less time over the ball could earn a European Tour player an additional $200k per season
2. Less time spent over the ball when putting, can lead to a 90% increase in a player having a positive Strokes Gained putting number, at the end of the round
3. Consistency of time spent over the ball increases the chance that a player will make the cut by 50%

I've got a link to this study on the resources page on the website.

To test and improve the consistency of your Pre Shot Routine, try timing it with a stopwatch during practice.

Although you are about to hear plenty of ideas for how to engage and be athletic before you start your swing, you'll need to find out what works for you and practice it, so it can be done in 10-15 seconds.

Target Retention and Visualization

One of the things that makes golf harder than other target sports is the fact that you are not looking at the target when you swing the club. When you throw a basketball, for example, you can see the target at the same time as you throw the ball. Your focus is on your target, not on your body, which makes it a lot easier. In golf, you're looking at the ball, not the target when you're playing your shot. For this reason, visualization and target retention helps because it imprints that image of where the target is and how the ball will get there in your mind. It's as close to facing the target while you're swinging as possible. Target focus keeps you athletic and reactive, instead of your mind wandering to less productive things while you're over the ball. Tiger Woods says that he can still "see" the image of the shot and the target in his mind while he's looking down at the ball.

When I evaluate a student's mental game during a playing lesson, I'm keen to find out for how long they can hold onto the image of the shot and/or target. With that image (or specific parts of it) being a key driver of the swing, it can really help them hit better shots. I ask them at what point do they lose the image of the shot and target. Is it over the ball, during the swing or after the shot? Was the visual image of the shot the same while over the ball as the one they saw in the rehearsal phase?

If you are a coach, you can challenge your student's ability to stay focused on the target by trying to distract them from it. Tiger Woods' father Earl Woods used to do this by dropping his bag and doing other things to distract Tiger when he was about to start his swing. You can do the same, and even mention an area that the player would want to avoid – a distraction that some players struggle with during the athletic phase. This is good practice for strengthening a player's focus.

Being Aware of Tension

Consistency of grip pressure and muscle tension is key for a consistent swing. For this reason, it's important to be aware of any additional tension in your hands and body. You'll often see Tour players relaxing their fingers on the grip and hanging their arms loose to make sure there's little tension in the hands and arms. You can increase this awareness during practice.

Hit some shots focusing only on grip pressure and arm tension (from my experience this is where players get the most changes in tension during a round). Find out what number out of 10 (1 being very light and 10 being very tight), produces your best shots. Once you've worked on this, you can make this a check in your Pre Shot Routine on the course. Focusing on the feel of your grip pressure is another way to keep your focus away from your thoughts and on something external which will help you play better shots.

Another way to stay relaxed and in the present is through your feet. You will notice some Tour players shuffle their feet before they start their swing (Louis Oosthuizen and Patrick Cantlay come to mind). Moving your feet (or other body parts) can move energy away from the hands and keep them relaxed, and if you focus on how your feet feel it will keep you present. Dr. Bob Rotella calls this having "Happy Feet".

Focus on Your Breathing

Some players find that they benefit from focusing on breathing before they start their swing. We will discuss the power of breathing as a stress management tool in the next module, but it's also powerful in keeping the mind quiet and focused. Try this for a "trigger" to start your backswing. During your last look at the target (while looking at the target and/or visualizing the shot), take a deep inhale through your nose. Then, as you move your eyes back to the ball, exhale slowly through your mouth. At the end of the exhale, start your backswing.

This is adapted from a breathing technique for archery, which helps the archer stay calm, centered and focused before shooting. By taking a nice deep inhale, you also get sufficient oxygen to your brain and to the muscles to make a nice fluid swing.

Focusing on Feel

As we discussed during the section on the Rehearsal Phase, knowing what a shot will feel like, can really help you if you're more of a "kinesthetic" player. This could be the feel of the whole swing or the impact position you want to get to. What is it that you want to feel in the swing? What will be the feeling in your hands for the shot you are about to play? Jordan Spieth says that when he's over the ball and doing his waggles, he's "feeling" the shot in his hands. For me personally, especially during the short game and putting, I'm imagining what impact will feel while I'm over the ball.

Focusing on Sound/Tempo

If you're more "auditory", sound is the sense that will keep your athletic mind engaged. For this reason, you'll benefit from imagining the tempo and rhythm of the shot.

Some players benefit from putting their swing to beats - for the take-away, top of backswing and downswing. They hear these beats before they start their swing.

Experiment with hearing the sound of the shot before you hit it. Is it a hard "smash" of a drive or is it a softer sound for a shot around the green. The imagined sound can connect with the athletic mind and help you produce it during the shot.

Another way to stay present and get away from thinking is using the sounds around you. Wait until you hear 2 different sounds before you start your swing. These could be birds chirping or the wind in the trees. Again, this will enable you to keep your focus external and not get distracted by your thoughts.

Using Words or Action Phrases

If you're more verbal, you can create a positive feeling and the desired movement through words. Verbal cues (or Self Talk) can be instructional, motivational, or rhythmical. Instructional cues are words that remind you of what you are supposed to do, such as "Focus", "Commit", "Breathe", "Be Athletic", "Balanced", "Free", etc. Motivational cues are phrases that can create emotion such as "You've got this!", or "Let's do this!" "This can go in…", "Calm and confident". Rhythmical cues are words that can help you create the right rhythm in the swing such as "Smooth and powerful" or "Super Smooth". In a recent interview, Adam Scott said that his swing thoughts are usually words which remind him of a nice smooth rhythm. He sometimes uses words such as "Inbee" (Inbee Park) or "Ernie" (Ernie Els) which reminds him to make a slow backswing and have a good rhythm.

Counting

Counting during the Athletic Phase of the Pre Shot Routine can serve the purpose of occupying the prefrontal cortex (the thinking part of the brain). This prevents you from being distracted by things that will affect your commitment to the shot and the fluidity of your swing. Try different counting sequences when you are over the ball. They can be simple, i.e., 1, 2, 3, 4, or if you require more "distraction" from thinking, sequences that involve multiplication such as 9, 18, 27, 36, etc.

"Quiet Eye"

The term "Quiet Eye" was coined by Professor Joan Vickers, a specialist in Kinesiology (the study of body movement), who conducted several studies in the '90s on the effects of how the eyes are used when performing an athletic task. During these studies, she found that higher-level players had a more consistent pattern of fixation of their eyes, which helped their performance.

During a study on the effects of eye movement in golf, she had players of varying ability levels wear a device which showed their "gaze" during a putting challenge.

Her studies concluded that better putters had a more consistent gaze between the ball and the target (and during a putt), whereas a novice was more erratic in their gaze pattern.

The "quieter" your eyes, the quieter (and more focused) your mind.

Sam Vines and Matt Wilson conducted a study at the University of Exeter, which drew the same conclusion: the use of the eyes is an important factor in how the body moves, especially during putting and the short game.

Vines says that *"there is a small window for the motor system to receive information from the eyes"*. It's your brain which interprets the messages from the eyes and organizes it into movement.

The results of their studies showed that not only was putting performance improved when golfers were trained in Quiet Eye but putting under pressure improved too.

How To Practice Quiet Eye

While you're practicing your putting, practice the focus of your eyes during the process and make it consistent. Try this:

- Back of ball and target
- Back of ball and target
- Back of ball

- Make stroke, focusing on back of ball and holding eyes in that position after the ball has been struck (not following ball)

Physical or "Kinesthetic" Swing Cues

A lot of players like to give themselves a moving/dynamic start to their swing, instead of being static. This can help you make an athletic movement during your swing and prevent freezing over the ball. Examples of these are:

- Sam Snead cocked his head to the left to start his swing, which was later copied by Jack Nicklaus
- Tom Kite and Nick Faldo, bend their knees slightly before starting their swing
- Gary Player kicks in his right knee
- Louis Oosthuizen and Patrick Cantlay shuffle their feet
- Greg Norman sets the toe of the club at the ball and then slides it forward before starting this swing
- Bryson DeChambeau does something similar and bounces the club before moving it behind the ball
- Harvey Penick told us in his "Little Red Book" that the back-swing should be started with a gentle forward press of the hands
- Rickie Fowler and Matt Kuchar hover the club
- Plenty of players waggle the club

Experiment with these many different things you can focus on during the Athletic Phase of the Pre Shot Routine, to get you ready for making the best swing or stroke possible.

Pre Shot Routine Exercise:
Use the information in Module 3 along with the drills in the Golf State of Mind Practice Book to build your Pre Shot Routine for each type of shot (Full Shot, Short Game Shot and Putt) and what you do in each of the phases of it (Planning, Rehearsal, Athletic). Update the Process Goals sheet which you printed out after Module 2.

Step 6: The Shot

Although the transition from the Athletic Phase to the swing needs to be swift and "reactive", the mind will need to focus on *something* during the swing. What you choose to focus on during the second or so it takes to swing will influence your movement and the outcome of the shot.

I'm sure you've experienced days where you played some of your best golf while not thinking about the technical aspects of your swing. But on the other hand, you might have had great rounds where you had a technical cue or "swing thought".

Even the best players in the world, who have very automatic and efficient swings, might have some awareness of their movement. In this section, I'd like to explore the different types of swing thoughts and help you find out what is best for you. In addition to the countless conversations that I've had with my students on the subject, I've taken a look at all the available research out there to come up with these opinions. I would also like to say that in this section I'm referring to focus during the full-swing, not the short game and putting which in my opinion should always be done without conscious awareness of your movement.

Types of Swing Thoughts

Firstly, the word "thoughts" is misleading as there shouldn't be any "thinking" or problem solving going on during your swing.

"Swing thoughts" should really be thought of as where your attention is during your swing or as your "swing focus". This swing focus could be on any number of things, such as a feel, a word, or awareness of a body part. Like everything with the mental game of golf, there is no *best* thing to focus on for all players - it's an individual preference that requires experimentation and self-discovery. First, let's take a look at what the research tells us.

Perhaps the most extensive and well-known studies on attentional focus in sports were done by Dr. Gabrielle Wulf, a Professor of Kinesiology at the University of Nevada.

Dr. Wulf's studies tested the effect on performance of 2 types of Swing Thoughts: "Internal Focus" which is focusing more on the body movement itself and "External

Focus", which is focusing on something outside of the body, such as the target or the club movement.

She concluded:

"Instructions that induce an external focus of attention, whereby attention is directed to the movement's effect on the environment, can enhance learning. Such instructions have been shown to be more effective than those that induce an internal focus by directing attention to the movements themselves." (Wulf, 2001)

In 2007, she performed a full-shot test on both novice and expert golfers, to see which type of focus was better for golfers of varying ability levels. Each ability group was randomly divided into two groups, and one performed the test by external focus (focusing on the club movement) and the other either by internal focus (focusing on a body part such as the arms), or what they normally do. The results showed significantly better performance by the external focus group.

Why would "External Focus" Be Better than "Internal Focus"?

Dr. Wulf's studies concluded that external focus facilitated greater "automaticity in movement control", that is, because the movement is done without focusing on it, it's more fluid. She said that: *"directing attention to one's movement (internal focus), tends to result in conscious control that constrains the motor system, which disrupts automaticity and causes superfluous muscle activity. In addition, internal focus tends to cause focus on the self which causes worry about one's performance and "micro-choking". When you are externally focused, you use more automatic control processes, which are unconscious and faster, making the movement more efficient, smoother, fluid and accurate."*

External Focus

Let's take a look at some examples of external focus:

- Focusing on the clubface
- Focusing on exactly where on the ball you will hit it – a quadrant or dimple on the ball (this can help you with path direction and strike)
- Focusing on how the club will connect with the ground after impact
- Focusing on your connection with the ground (through your feet)
- Swinging to the target or to "first base"
- Swinging the weight of the club with light grip pressure
- Staying in balance
- The flight of the ball i.e., the trajectory and shape (known as distal external focus)
- Tiger Woods says he has an awareness of what the clubface is doing in his swing (through the feel in his hands)
- Tiger also said that he is able to retain the image of the target and the shot in his mind during this swing (like he's taken a mental photo of it)

How does the body know what to do when focus is external?

One might argue that external focus should work well for a Tour player, but players of a lower skill level would be better off thinking about their swings to get into the correct positions.

However, studies show that with an external goal, your "athletic mind" already knows a lot of what to do to achieve that goal and can "self-organize" your body's movement.

Fred Shoemaker of Extraordinary Golf came up with an interesting way to demonstrate this and train his students to swing the club more efficiently: He has them throw the club to the target! Interestingly, when the focus is on throwing the club as far as possible, the body uses its natural intelligence to assume the correct positions of the golf swing (using the weight of the clubhead and swinging with an in-to-out path). So, if the body already knows what it needs to do to swing the club, then internal focus can inhibit it.

From my experience of working with golfers of all levels over the past 15 years, I would agree that being externally focused during the swing is generally better, but I would stop before making a blanket statement that *all* players are better off with it.

Internal Focus

Internal focus is certainly helpful during "Block Practice" when you are developing technical skill working on technique. However, some players can find it effective on the course for the following reasons:

- It keeps your mind focused on one simple thing instead of it wandering from shot to shot
- It can remind you to focus on a specific movement that can increase your chance of a good shot
- It can help prevent you reverting to old habits when you are under pressure
- It can help make swing changes permanent
- If you believe it's the key to good shots, it can give you confidence in your swing

Types of "Internal" focus

Here's are some examples of internal focus as used by The World's top players:

- Rory McIlroy says that making a wide takeaway is key for him with the driver
- Justin Thomas says he tries to "cover" the ball with his chest as he turns through impact[1]
- Paul Casey says his swing thought is maintaining his posture and making a wide takeaway
- Patrick Cantlay says his swing thought is to have a smooth transition
- Adam Scott says he focuses on getting onto his left side through impact

---

[1] Source https://golf.com/instruction/pga-tour-player-swing-thought/ Luke Kerr-Dineen

- Graeme McDowell says that during those first three feet of the swing he makes sure the clubhead works away wide and outside his hands
- Dustin Johnson and Collin Morikawa make sure their left arm stays close to their chest on the backswing for their irons

These internal swing thoughts might not be what that player currently uses, but it's what they said at the time they were interviewed.

Although simple internal focus can have benefits, problems arise when it becomes too specific and varied from shot to shot. Unfortunately, the abundance of information freely available on the swing and data from launch monitors, can cause information overload, and the player will try to self-diagnose after every shot, making them more and more internal and focusing too much on specific movements. If there is too much self-instruction, especially before swinging, it can create anxiety and disconnection from the intention for the shot. Additionally, the movement is no longer whole or "holistic", so it loses its fluidity and timing. If you do have an internal swing focus, make it simple, broad and consistent e.g., making a good turn as opposed to thinking about your wrist angle at the top of your backswing.

Learning Style and Personality Traits

While you are examining what swing thoughts are best for you, you will want to consider your learning style or "personality traits".

Golf coach Dr. Noel Rousseau wanted to test Dr. Gabrielle Wulf's conclusions further and in an 8 year study he set out to see whether golfers would play better with no swing thoughts at all. He tested this hypothesis with a group of golfers of advanced ability level (all were less than a 6 handicap).

During testing, he had each player follow a routine for each full shot they hit on the course. For the first part of their Pre Shot Routine, they were allowed to follow their normal routine, and if they wanted to have a swing thought in their rehearsal swings, they could. But as they walked into the ball, all players had to stop "thinking" (he called it the "Flow Drill") and the rest of the shot routine was simple – they put their feet in place, while not being overly concerned about alignment, and as soon as the club went behind the ball, they started their swing quickly with no thought about it at all.

The results showed that some players in the group improved using this method, while others did not. So why would this be?

Upon further testing of each player, Rousseau concluded that personality traits were a factor in whether the "no swing thought" routine worked, or not.

His findings suggested that more verbal learners/communicators (who could also be referred "left brain" dominant) were better with some sort of internal instruction.

More visual learners/communicators (who could be referred to as "right brain dominant") were better with little conscious awareness of their movement and more external focus.

The likely reason for this is that verbal learners are used to processing information by talking to themselves about it, whereas visual learners need to see things in pictures.

You could think of a verbal, logical learner/thinker as being someone like Bryson DeChambeau compared with an intuitive, visual thinker/learner such as Bubba Watson.

Dr. Rousseau took the study a step further and added pressure to the test by giving prizes for successful outcomes. His main conclusion was that of those players who were better with a swing thought, those with a broader internal focus performed better than those with more detailed internal focus when put under pressure.

Kinesthetic Focus

From my experience, Kinesthetic focus or "feel" is probably the most common swing focus among elite players. There's no one swing thought; instead, it's about creating a feel for the unique shot that they are about to hit. The rehearsal swing is used for creating that feel and then they have that in mind during the swing. This would be rehearsing and imagining the feel of certain parts of the swing such as the feeling of a good shoulder turn, the feel of the downswing for the shot they are intending to hit, or the feel of impact.

Auditory Focus

Some players benefit from an auditory or sound focus during the swing. This allows them to control their tempo and timing of the swing.

Let's start by defining "tempo", which is:

the ratio of the time taken to get to the top of the backswing to the time taken to get back to the ball.

If you can make this consistent, then you will have a consistent swing.

Tempo is important as it determines the timing and sequencing of the swing and brings together the many moving parts to get to a consistent impact position. When we get nervous on the golf course or if we start hitting a few bad shots, one of the first things to be affected is tempo. When your timing is inconsistent, your shots will be too. Although a tempo swing focus can benefit all types and levels of players, it could be even more effective for players who are more "auditory".

Examples of tempo swing thoughts are songs, music, beats or counts that you can play in your mind during your swing. Experiment with a tempo that fits your swing e.g., a 1-2-3 for the backswing and 1 for the downswing. Counting by itself is a good "neutral" swing focus to keep your mind free of thoughts that could interfere with your swing.

An anticipation of what the shot will sound like can also help players who are more auditory.

Using Words during the swing

In his book, "The Inner Game of Golf", Timothy Gallwey popularized the "Back-hit" method, which is saying the word "back" on the back-swing and "hit" on the down-swing. The purpose of it is to occupy the "thinking-self", so the "athletic-self" is free to make the swing without conscious thought about it. For more verbal learners, you can experiment with different words that can help create a desired movement, such as "smooth back, powerful through". You could also say something that helps with your timing, such as saying any 3-syllable word during your backswing.

Swing Thoughts Under Pressure

When we are feeling pressure, it can cause us to get more internal with our focus and try to control the swing. At this time, it's even more important to stay connected with the target and be athletic in your swing. Try to keep your focus external or on very simple and broad movements.

What are your tendencies under pressure? Do you get quick and tighten your grip pressure? If so, you will want to think of your swing as being long, slow, and loose. PGA Tour player Keegan Bradley says one of his favorite swing cues is keeping his facial muscles relaxed.

He says: *"When you can get your mouth to relax, your whole body relaxes."* (Source: Golf Digest)

Neutral Swing Thoughts

Neutral swing thoughts are for keeping your mind distracted during the swing (with things that don't necessarily relate to the process of hitting the shot), so you don't attempt to control your movement, or focus on anything that will interfere with fluidity of the swing.

- Humming a song
- Counting
- Breathing in on the back-swing and out on the down-swing (this can also help with timing)

Self-coaching and Making Adjustments

If you know exactly what causes your misses, you can "self-coach" and make adjustments to your swing during your rounds. Some players will plan for it in their pre-round preparation – so they have the solutions ready for their known misses. This can avoid searching for the answers with each swing. To make these subtle swing changes on the course, use your rehearsal swings to focus on the change but keep the focus broad/minimal during the actual swing. You will want to avoid forcing the club into different positions during your swing.

In summary...
- External focus is generally better than internal, especially under pressure
- Internal swing thoughts can work but they should be simple and broad to keep the swing "whole"

- Avoid switching between different swing thoughts with every swing
- Know your misses and plan for adjustments

Swing Thought Exercise:
Using what you've learned in this lesson, write down your current Swing Thoughts (for Full Shots) and add it to the Process Goals Sheet you printed out in Module 2.

Step 7: The Post Shot Routine

> *"Between stimulus and response there is a space. In that space is our power to choose our response. In our response lies our growth and our freedom."*
> **- Victor Frankl**

In the final phase of the Shot Routine, we need to choose the best way to respond to *any* outcome that might have occurred, end the shot and move on. Good shots are easy to move on from, but less desirable outcomes can leave us feeling frustrated, angry, and disappointed. Letting those emotions take hold can affect how well we play the next shot. For this reason, we need to be aware of our emotions and take the necessary action to move forward and return to the present, so we can bring the best version of ourselves to the upcoming shot.

As I've said before, the greatest value of the game of golf is not trophies and scores, but what it teaches us about ourselves to become better human beings. One of these times we get to practice a key life skill is after a shot. Short game guru James Sieckmann calls the time after a bad shot "the most important 5 seconds in golf". How well you are able to deal with setbacks on the golf course, is a reflection of how you are able to deal with them in your life. Let's take a look at how we can get better at it and use those experiences to grow as a player and as a person.

Accepting "bad" shots

"I can prepare before a shot, and then that's it. From there whatever happens, happens."
– Scottie Scheffler

Golf is a difficult game. If it wasn't, you probably wouldn't enjoy it as much. Undesirable outcomes and what we call "bad" shots are an inevitable part of every round for all levels of player. That said, I recommend that you don't call them "bad" - they are simply a part of the game that every golfer has to deal with. Good golf is not about hitting every shot perfectly. Ben Hogan famously said that he only hit 5-6 perfect shots in any round, the rest were good misses. Of course, the intention is always to hit good shots, but accepting that you will probably miss-hit some is important in controlling your responses to them. Accept your misses before you go out to play.

Mistakes and failure are not to be feared or thought of as wrong, they are to be accepted and seen as an integral part of getting better. That is how we create the freedom to play well and the mental toughness to work our way through challenges.

Choosing A Response Instead of Reacting

"Champions respond to what happens, losers react"

However you feel after a shot, it is acceptable. You can't control your primary emotional response to any outcome or situation - it is what it is. That said, you *do* have control over what happens immediately after it and whether you allow it to affect your mood and the rest of the round.

E.g., If you miss a short putt or hit your drive OB, you can expect to feel disappointed or frustrated. This is perfectly normal. The key is to notice it and accept it. Once you do that, you get the control to decide what to do next.

But without awareness of how you are feeling and thinking, that primary emotion can trigger negative self talk and secondary emotions such as anger, shame and fear. Your whole mood and outlook can change for the worse.

Instead of reacting with swearing or beating yourself up, try simply observing how you feel. Fred Shoemaker, the author of "Extraordinary Golf" says that *"the few seconds after a shot is when you need to be the most aware of your emotions."*

Being able to notice thoughts and emotions and then pause before choosing how to respond is something that takes practice.

Storing memories of shots

As we discussed earlier in the program, the brain has an innate "negativity bias". For our ancient brain, it's more important to remember where threats to our survival are and to predict upcoming danger than to think about potential rewards.

For this reason, it stores negative events as memories more deeply than it does positive ones. These memories can then trigger negative emotions in the future. E.g., if you have lots of bad memories of missing 3ft putts, then more "negative" emotions are going to be triggered when you have 3ft putts in the future.

For the most part, the brain's negative bias is not helpful to us. In fact, we need to do our best to reverse it as much as possible and give more weight to positive events. By doing so, more positive emotions will be triggered in association with different situations in your game, instead of negative ones.

After a good shot, anchor it and hold onto that feeling of the swing and the emotion you feel for as long as possible. By doing so you'll store the memory of it. Your anchor could be an action, like a fist pump or a word that you say to yourself. We also do this reinforcing of positives in the Post Round Review (which we'll get to later).

Conversely, undesirable outcomes/shots need to be let go of quickly, so they are not stored in our memory. Try the following techniques to help you do it.

Module 3: The Shot Routine

Be your best friend and best coach
> *"Being negative on the golf course is a habit. You hit a shot and complain about it, and that's just the way you play golf. [The turning point for me] was going from being generally not very nice to myself on the golf course to being quite nice to myself on the golf course."*
> **– 2006 US Open Champion, Geoff Ogilvy**

What is the best thing to say to yourself after a bad shot? It's always going to feel disappointing, but why layer negative self talk on top of it? What would a good coach say to you? They're certainly not going to be critical and pessimistic. Be self-compassionate in those moments when you feel the pain of a bad shot, don't make it worse with negative self talk. Try something like: *"It's done now, nothing can be done about it now. Be strong and get ready for the next shot"*, or be curious and ask yourself, *"what can I learn from that shot"* (without overanalyzing it)?

You might find it better to recover from a poor shot by being firmer with yourself. Players such as Jordan Spieth and Tiger Woods can sometimes give themselves a talking to and tell themselves they can do better. Reflect, experiment and find and the approach or language would be best for you.

Take a positive from *every* shot
This is a tough challenge after some shots, but it will help you keep a positive mindset and train you to be

more optimistic. After each shot ask yourself: *"What did I do well and what was good about that shot?"*

Count to 10
Putting 10 seconds of time between the way the shot made you feel, and your next move will allow you to respond positively. Tiger Woods has a "ten pace rule", where after he hits a disappointing shot, he allows himself 10 paces to vent and process it, before he puts it behind him.

Use Humor
> *"Realizing bad shots happen is the best way to deal with them. Take the drama out of the shank or top. Use humor or laughter to make it go away, and then move on."*
>
> **– Zach Johnson**

As we will discuss in the next module, using facial expressions such as smiling can trick your brain into producing feel good chemicals which can give you a lift after a disappointing shot.

Use A Post Shot Trigger
Do something that ends the shot and puts it behind you such as the action of putting the club back in the bag or taking off your glove.

Evaluate the shot
The first thing to ask yourself when reviewing a shot is: *"did I achieve my process goals?"*

If the answer is *"no"*, then highlighting which of them you missed and making it a priority for the next shot is important.

Were you committed? How good was your tempo? Did you pick a good target? Noticing these things will only help.

As we discussed previously, if there's a pattern to your misses, (and you know you're swing well enough), you can make the necessary adjustments to change the pattern.

"Erase and Replace"
Say the word "Erase" and then use your imagination to replay the shot in the way you would have liked.

Post Shot Routine Exercise:
Using what you've learned in this module, write down your Post Shot Routine and add it to the Process Goals Sheet.

Module 4: Playing Fearless Golf

> *"I think the reason I won so many majors, was because in my mind they were easier to win than a regular tournament. The pressure affected me in a positive way, whereas for a lot of my opponents, it affected them in a negative way. I knew I had the advantage."*
> – Jack Nicklaus

What is Pressure?
Pressure comes from the mind in situations where you *perceive* the stakes to be high and there is some chance of failure or not making the most of an opportunity. On the one side there is the excitement from the possibility of success and gain, and on the other is the fear of failure and loss. The magnitude of pressure you feel and how it affects you, comes down to:

- How your mind has been conditioned in the past to respond to potential threats or fears
- How you can control your mind to respond to how you are thinking and feeling when the pressure is on

What is Fear?

The mind's primary role is to keep us safe and away from threats to our survival, more than it is to make us happy. From the moment we're born and throughout our lives, the mind is conditioned by our environment and puts things that (we know or believe) could harm us, to memory. The mind is always looking for patterns, and when it predicts a threat, it automatically triggers physiological changes within us to make us move away from that potential danger. The fear response is a necessary part of being human and it's designed to protect us, but at the same time it can limit us from becoming the best we can be. We are all, to some extent, driven by our fears.

In her book, "Fear Less: How to Win at Life Without Losing Yourself", Performance Psychologist and Culture Coach Dr. Pippa Grange tells us that there are two types of fear, "In The Moment Fear" and "Pervasive Fear".

"In The Moment Fear" are the thoughts and feelings that arise in the moment when you experience fear. Pervasive Fear is a deeper, underlying fear of not being good enough, fear of what other people think, or a fear of failure. Let's start with two of the most common Pervasive Fears: Fear of What Others Think and Fear of Failure.

Fear of What Others Think

With us humans being social creatures, it's part of our nature to care about what others will think of us. Let's take the example of one of the most common fears in this respect, public speaking. What's interesting is that there is no physical danger involved in giving a bad speech, but many people are terrified by it and avoid public speaking at all costs. The reason for this, psychologists believe, is that we fear losing our standing within the "tribe". I use the word "tribe" here, because fear of what others think evolved in humans hundreds of thousands of years ago. Not only was the success of the tribe vital to our survival but our place within the tribe was too. Weaker members of the tribe were often excluded from it, making it harder for those individuals to survive. Fear of public speaking and other activities that can expose us socially is our ancient brains at work. We innately want to be seen as being a valued member of the "tribe" (or community) and therefore we don't want to risk exclusion by appearing weak. We fear social disapproval and not "being good enough", which in golf can make us afraid of:

- Poor performances and high scores
- Disappointing parents and coaches
- Judgment from other players or peers
- Not being selected for the team or letting the team down
- Choking

What also makes this type of fear worse in our modern world is the transparency of our results. For early humans, the tribe was small compared to today's "social networks", where for better or worse, our successes and failures can be seen by hundreds, if not thousands of people. I see this type of fear exacerbated more in younger players, but with the increased use of social media among all ages, many of us are conditioned to care more about how we look to others.

Fear of Failure

Many golfers fear not living up to their "potential", not achieving their goals or keeping up with their peers. They might have long-term goals they've been working towards for years such as playing college or professional golf, breaking a certain score, or winning a championship. The fear of not achieving that goal when the opportunity arises or not having their best game show up in the big moments, can negatively affect many players.

In The Moment Fear

In The Moment Fear is how the moment makes you feel and think, such as feeling shaky over a putt and thinking *"don't miss this putt"* or being nervous that you'll hit a poor shot with people watching you tee off. Think of a situation that you fear and immediately a movie will play in your mind and change the way you feel inside. What you are experiencing here is In The Moment Fear – your heart rate increasing, racing thoughts and physical tension.

In this Module, I'd like to show you how you can become a Champion golfer by learning how to change your relationship with your Pervasive Fears and respond in the best possible way to In the Moment Fear.

What Are Your Fears?

In your notebook, write down your answers to these questions:

> *What do you think your "Pervasive Fears" are?*
> *What have they prevented you from doing in the past?*
> *How can they affect you and your golf game?*
> *What do you consider failure in your rounds/tournaments?*
> *Is there a better way to perceive and deal with this failure?*
> *What thoughts and feelings can arise in the pressure moments?*

The Two Minds

> *"In a very real sense we have two minds, one that thinks and one that feels."*
> **- Daniel Goleman, author of the book Emotional Intelligence**

To go a step deeper in understanding our Pervasive and In the Moment Fears, it's important to distinguish between the "conscious" and "subconscious" minds.

How we automatically react and feel in a situation is determined by the "feeling" or "subconscious" mind.

These responses are learned and ingrained throughout our lives. The conscious mind is our awareness of what is happening and how we "consciously" direct our attention in response to how we feel.

To illustrate this, let's take a look at something that psychologists call "The Behavior Cycle", which you can see in the diagram below:

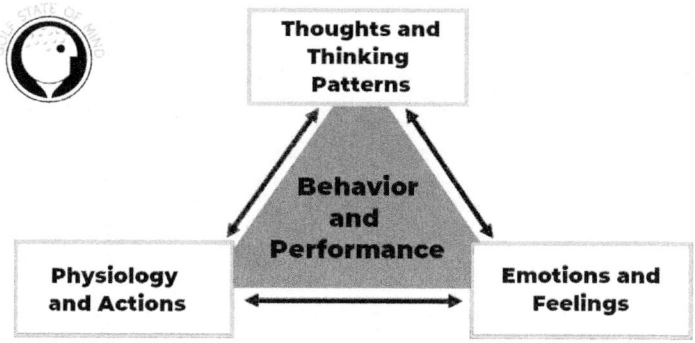

The Behavior Cycle tells us that how we behave and perform is determined by how we think, manage our feelings and emotions and act physically.

Let's start with how thinking patterns are formed, and how we can change them to reduce Pervasive Fear and improve performance.

The Two Minds

If I was to ask you what "thinking" is, you might refer to it as using your brain to solve a problem or to "think about" something.

In his book "Thinking Fast and Slow", psychologist and Nobel Prize winner, Daniel Kahneman explains that most of our decisions are made using what he calls "System 1" or the automatic, intuitive mind. The logical and analytical mind, which he calls "System 2" is used very little in comparison.

The Conscious Mind

Kahneman says that when you are doing a Sudoku puzzle or a multiplication problem such as 14 x 12 = ???, you are (mostly) using your analytical mind or System 2. It's objective and factual, not based on our previous experiences or beliefs.

Focusing on the words on this page as you read them is a conscious decision. You are directing your conscious attention towards this and only this (although your level of awareness determines how focused you really are). However, how you feel and "think" about what you are reading is not a conscious decision – it's a predetermined automatic response from your "Subconscious Mind".

The Subconscious Mind

The subconscious mind is where our memories are stored and the rules for all our mental and physical processes. In fact, neuroscientists say that up to 95 % of our mental and physiological processes are subconscious or automatic. We are born with the body's biological processes, but most of our mental processes are learned and conditioned over time.

The reason that the subconscious mind is used to do most of our "thinking" is about speed and energy efficiency – it's faster and uses less energy to operate than the conscious mind. Remember that the mind's primary role is to keep us safe and alive. If the energy-intensive analytical mind or "system 2" was required to do all our thinking, we would be unproductive, tired, and we wouldn't be able to respond quickly if threatened.

How The Subconscious Mind Works

Neuroscientists are still trying to figure out exactly how the subconscious mind works, but here's what we do know. The subconscious mind is taking a snapshot of every moment you live (through the window of the conscious mind/where you direct your attention) and storing those memories so it can do the best possible job at predicting what's going to happen next and protect you from danger if needed. This is why the brain has a "negativity bias" and stores negative experiences more deeply than it does good ones, to protect us from them in the future.

Being more alert to danger than rewards helped humans survive under harsh conditions hundreds of thousands of years ago. But even in our relatively safe modern world, the human mind still works in this way. We instinctively see threats more than we do potential rewards. Although negative thinking is a normal part of being human, it doesn't mean that we have to accept it. When we focus too much on our negative experiences, use negative self talk, or focus too much about what could go wrong, we reinforce and continue negative thinking patterns.

You can think of the subconscious mind as a storyteller which creates patterns of thinking using something that's called "Associative Memory". I.e., if a situation was dangerous in the past, it will automatically respond to prepare you for it if you face it again. If it was joy that you experienced, then that situation (or memory of it) can trigger that same feeling/emotion by "association". It's the subconscious mind that "feels". What we do, experience and think "consciously" affects how we automatically think and feel in the future.

Take this very simple example of association (from the book "Thinking Fast and Slow"). If you were to see a photo of a dinner table and then you were asked to fill in the blanks of the word "S_ _P", you are more likely to fill in "SOUP", than if you were to see a picture of a shower, in which case you would probably fill in the blanks to create the word "SOAP".

In this simple example, because you've ingrained the association of bathroom and soap and dinner table and food many times before, the connection is made quickly in your subconscious mind without you having to use the analytical mind.

The subconscious is constantly linking memories of the past to interpret the present and create expectations of the future (which it does automatically for all our waking hours).

Because it's the subconscious or "feeling" mind which links one thought to another (our thinking patterns) and triggers our feelings and behaviors, it means that we must be mindful about what we allow into it. By being selective about the inputs, we will get more of the outputs that are conducive to better performance and overall wellbeing.

The Conscious Mind is The Gateway to The Subconscious

What we consciously choose to focus on or "think about" can become a pattern, and the more we do it, the more that pattern becomes ingrained and a part of who we are.

An example of conscious thinking that becomes a subconscious thinking pattern or "habit", is driving a car. After consciously learning the correct way to drive a car and obey traffic rules, you do it more and more automatically to the point where it requires very little use of your analytical mind. E.g., When you see your turn approaching, you no longer consciously think to yourself, *"I should indicate now, press the brake pedal and start turning the steering wheel",* you just do it. Even though there is "thinking" involved, you are not aware of it happening and you automatically get the physical action of indicating, pressing the brake pedal and turning the steering wheel at the right time. You've created a "thinking pattern".

When we are practicing a physical skill such as golf, we are consciously deciding on what we focus on as we prepare to hit a shot and during the swing, so that (over time) the correct way to set up and swing becomes more automatic and "subconscious". The subconscious mind is remembering which neural circuits need to be fired to activate the muscles required to perform a specific movement.

In his book "The Talent Code", Daniel Coyle says that the more these neural circuits are used, the more they are strengthened by a protein called "Myelin". He says:

"Every human movement, thought or feeling is a precisely timed electric signal traveling through a chain of neurons – a circuit of nerve fibers. Myelin is the insulation that wraps these nerve fibers and increases signal strength, speed and accuracy. The more we fire a particular circuit, the more myelin optimizes that circuit, and the stronger, faster, and more fluent our movements and thoughts become."

Every day, for better or worse, we are "priming" the subconscious to create patterns of thinking and associations with different stimuli.

A good example of priming for golf comes from one of the greatest golfers of all time, Jack Nicklaus. Jack famously said: *"I never missed a putt in my mind"*. Despite people saying to him that they saw him miss, he would always reply that he didn't. This might sound silly, but there's some sound logic to it. What he was doing, whether he knew it as such or not, was "priming" his subconscious mind so all he remembered was the putts he made. Over the years, he developed the belief that he was a player that made every putt, which gave him incredible confidence on the greens. It wasn't that he expected to make every putt and was disappointed when he didn't, it's that he chose not to focus on them, so he forgot about them as quickly as they happened.

The subconscious is always listening to what the conscious mind tells it (and what you allow your mind to focus on), which will affect whether you develop the winning traits of confidence and self-belief and become a fearless golfer.

Reducing Pervasive Fear

Pervasive Fears are more deep-rooted fears that have been conditioned by events throughout our lives. These fears can be triggered subconsciously, so it's important to try to pinpoint what yours are (we all have them) so you can begin working on reducing them.

Changing Thinking Patterns

Your System 1, or subconscious mind, quickly makes connections from one thought to another based on your experiences/memories and how you've *allowed* yourself to think over time. These are called "Thinking Patterns".

To change our relationship with our fears in the long-run, we need to recognize the thinking patterns that have made them Pervasive Fears.

These are most clear to see when we are under pressure, which is when we don't have as much capacity for directing thought, as more energy is being directed to the sympathetic nervous system (to protect us). This is another reason that playing under pressure is a win-win whatever the result, as you get to learn more about who you are and how you think.

Every day we are shaping our thinking for future performance (for better or worse). We can choose to listen to negative thoughts and reinforce them or change the patterns and improve performance.

This is where the "Inner Work" and learning better ways to think (that reverse the brain's negativity bias) can help. In his book "The Happiness Advantage", Shawn Achor tells us that because of "neuroplasticity" (the brain's ability to modify, change, and adapt), thinking patterns can be changed to help us be more positive, happier and mentally stronger. To start this process, we need to do some self-examination, so we can identify our fears and negative thinking patterns and replace them when they appear. So instead of continuing a negative storyline, you'll create new positive thinking patterns which will guide you to your optimal performance state more often.

Step 1: Identification
The first step is to recognize what your fears and negative thinking patterns are. This isn't easy and requires vulnerability. Most of us don't confront our fears because of the discomfort that comes with thinking about them. It's easier to ignore them. By being more aware of what your fears are and what is at the source of your negative thinking, uncomfortable feelings and underperformance, you can start to do the inner work to overcome them.

What situations can make you feel uncomfortable and trigger negative thinking?
Write them out. It's easier to examine them when they are out in front of you, which is why writing in a journal is helpful. Examples are:

- Before a round (fear of shooting a high score)
- After hitting a poor shot (you fear another one)
- After a round (being overly critical)
- A tough shot or the first tee shot (you fear the negative outcome)
- Getting paired up with better players (you fear being the weaker player)
- Particular shots such as chips from tight lies
- A good score with a few holes left (fearing losing it)
- A bad start to the round
- A poor warm-up session (you fear that it will continue)

Step 2: Choose a better way to think

For each of the fear triggers you listed in Step 1, write down some of your negative thoughts around it and then a new, better way to think. Here are some examples:

Negative thinking pattern:

"I hate that first tee shot, it doesn't fit my shot shape and I always miss the fairway."

Better way to think:

"I'm going to conquer that first tee shot. I love challenges and I know that if I want to improve, I will need to learn how to play shots that don't fit my shot shape. I will decide on a good strategy and stay focused on my intention, not what I don't want to happen."

Negative thinking pattern:

"If I play like I did in my last round, I won't make the team. I have to shoot a good score.

Better way to think:

"I feel nervous that I won't make the team, but that is normal. I will choose to focus on my process and if I fail to make the team, I will learn valuable lessons to improve."

Negative thinking pattern:

What if I shoot a high score? What will they think of me?

Better way to think:

"It's possible I will succeed and do well. But If I don't, I can accept it as I know that Golf is not a reflection of who I am as a person. I'm going to focus on my values and player identity and accept the outcome whatever it will be."

Visualization to Overcome Fear

Another way to "prime" your mind to give you a green light to proceed in situations that can trigger fear, is Visualization.

By imagining how you would like to feel, think and behave in situations that have in the past made you

Module 4: Playing Fearless Golf

feel uncomfortable, can help you respond in that way when you are there again. By doing this, you create a story in your mind that you've been there before and succeeded, so by association, more positive responses will be triggered.

Visualization Exercise:
Imagine a situation that you know will make you feel fearful. It could be the first tee shot of a tournament, being right on the cut line, or playing with the lead with a few holes to go. Imagine the scenario vividly – the look of it, how you will feel inside, the sounds, etc.

How does that situation make you feel? What are the negative thoughts that can appear? What is your body language like? Feel the nerves arise and your heart rate increase. This might feel uncomfortable, but by understanding and facing your fears you will begin the process of letting them go.

Now I'd like you to imagine yourself succeeding. What are the thoughts, feelings and actions that you will have to do so?

How will you look? You can combine this moment of success with a "trigger", which is saying a word, clicking your fingers, tapping yourself, etc., which can be used in the real moments to trigger the same internal state. I'll discuss more about how to use triggers later in the module.

Create that movie of your success in the pressure moments with full effects and play it in your mind every day.

Self Awareness or "Mindfulness"

> *"Mindfulness is a pause - the space between stimulus and response - that's where choice lies."*
> **– Tara Brach**

Now that you know the thinking patterns that are unhelpful and continue a pattern of fear and underperformance, you will need to notice when you are repeating it. With more Self Awareness, you will notice and be able to change the negative thinking patterns that are being reinforced and make them more positive.

Our "ancient brain" is very good at focusing on negatives and telling us negative stories about our experiences or our weaknesses, which further commits them to memory. The negative storyteller is always at the door, but the good news is that you get to choose whether you open it and allow him in.

The rumination of negative thoughts and habit of telling yourself a negative story is what we know as "Performance Anxiety". This anxiety makes it harder to keep the mind in the present and instead it gets stuck in a negative thinking loop which becomes a negative state of mind. What's worse, is that most of the time we're not aware that we're doing it. The mind tells us stories and we just follow along and believe them.

What are some of your negative thinking patterns that you can have about your golf game? Some examples are:

"I'm just not cut out for this."
"I always shoot in the 80s in tournaments."
"I always play badly when it matters. I'm a choker."
"I started golf too late, these players learned how to play much younger."
"I will never be as good as him/her."

Research tells us that the most effective way to pull ourselves out of negative thinking patterns and notice how we're thinking is a practice called "Mindfulness".

The practice of mindfulness, allows us to:

- notice how we are feeling and thinking without identifying with it or reacting to it
- redirect or keep our focus on what's most important
- turn the volume down on "mental chatter"
- be more accepting of what we are experiencing, so we can be more agile in how we navigate challenges

Using Mindfulness to Sidestep Negative Thoughts
"Focus, notice and redirect"
  - Dr. Amishi Jha, author of Peak Mind

As we go about our days, feelings are being triggered by our environment (events, people, our senses, etc.) or by things that we consciously choose to focus on (or "think" about). Most of the 70,000 or so thoughts that we have each day are automatic, conditioned responses to feelings. The mind likes to create stories to give meaning to the way we feel. What might surprise you is that roughly two-thirds of our daily thoughts are "negative" and fearful perceptions of the past or future (it's the brain's survival mechanism at work).

The reality is that we are not our thoughts. Without cultivating awareness of the thoughts that surround our feelings, we can easily live them out and deepen the negative thinking patterns and habits that hold us back.

Awareness is about noticing what is actually happening in the moment and being able to direct your attention in the best way possible.

With mindfulness practice, you get to observe what the mind is doing, so you can pause between feelings and the thoughts that follow. You get to create some distance between feelings and thinking by observing them and separating "the self" from them. I.e., thinking and feelings are happening, but you are *not* the thinking or the feelings.

So instead of being "triggered" and reacting, we can choose what we focus on next. With practice and repetition, we gain more control of our emotions, behaviors and the habits we form.

This is an especially valuable skill in golf. In most other sports, the game happens faster - there's less time to be influenced by the thinking and stories that follow your feelings. But in golf, most of the time you're "playing", you're in between shots with plenty of time to let your thoughts interfere and further change how you feel and how you play.

Without awareness the mind will jump to conclusions and tell us unhelpful stories that are not based on reality – it's just doing its job (to protect us) but it puts us on an emotional rollercoaster.

Let's say you hit your first tee shot out of bounds. It is perfectly normal for feelings of disappointment and frustration to be triggered as you see your ball heading towards, and eventually landing O.B. But what follows next is up to you *if you are aware*. When we experience those feelings, the mind might create a story around it, such as "It's going to be a bad day", "What a terrible start this is", "How could this happen after hitting it great on the range?" or "How embarrassing is this?"

None of these thoughts are true but the more you listen to them, the more believable they become, and you are more likely to find emotions and behaviors in accordance with them. You are no longer acting in line with your player values and reality but reacting to whatever external outcome arises.

When you're more aware and "mindful", you'll be able to smile at the little voice in your head and gently shift your attention back to the present and the task at hand, without any judgment at all.

3 Steps to Greater Mindfulness
Zen master, Thich Nhat Hahn, said that the first step to being more mindful is acknowledging how you feel in the present. I.e. you say to yourself *"I feel _____"*, such as *"I feel nervous"*, or *"I feel angry"*. This is an act of acceptance and self-compassion. It's ok to experience a

feeling or thought and not try to change them. Feelings are temporary, not permanent. If you tell yourself that it's unacceptable and resist, you give them power. By noticing and accepting them, you allow them to pass, instead of them becoming tension and changing your mood.

Step 1: Acknowledge: What am I thinking and how am I feeling now? Be curious instead of judgmental =>

Step 2: Accept:
"I'm thinking____ and feeling_____, and that's ok. =>

Step 3: Reset
Bring yourself back to your breathing, smiling, or a positive affirmation, etc.

The more you go through this process, the more mindful you become. We can increase this awareness and control of our attention further, with a practice of daily meditation.

Mindfulness Meditation

Practicing meditation for as little as 5-10 minutes per day can help you:

- Become more mindful of your attention, so you can stay in the present and focused on a task for longer
- Let negative thoughts pass to lower stress and performance anxiety

- Improve self-control (by allowing you to pause and not be impulsive)
- Increase awareness of your feelings and behaviors
- Practice breathing

What is meditation?
Firstly, meditation is not what a lot of people think it is: It is *not* a challenge to see how long you can go without thinking. You're not failing if your mind wanders, instead you are succeeding if you *notice* it wander. Meditation is about becoming more aware of *where* your mind is, and through that practice, you increase your ability to stay present and focused on what you intend for longer. By being more of an observer of your thoughts and feelings, it gives you more self-control over your thoughts and emotions. It also gives you a look into your mind so you can observe what's there without judging it.

There are many different types of meditation, but all involve some sort of "anchor" for your focus for a specific length of time i.e., your breath, a mantra, or focusing on how your body feels.

Each time you notice your mind wandering away from your anchor, you gently bring your attention back to it. The more you're able to notice where your attention is at any time, the more you're improving your awareness and the more you'll stay in the present.

Training yourself to be more present is a very simple concept but a challenging exercise. The practice of meditation has been done for thousands of years, but it's been growing in popularity in recent years – probably because people are becoming more aware that they struggle to focus their attention, which is causing stress and underperformance.

The easiest way to get started is with a guided meditation app, such as Calm and Headspace, which provide guided meditations of 10-15 minutes each day.

You can meditate at any time of day, but studies suggest that it's best done first thing in the morning.

Here's how to get started:

1. Find a place where you won't be disturbed for 10-15 minutes and silence your phone
2. Start your guided meditation or calming sounds/music
3. Sit comfortably with a straight back, place your hands gently in your lap or by your sides, and close your eyes
4. Start by inhaling through your nose for 4 seconds until you feel your belly go out, which gives it the name "deep belly breathing". If only your chest is moving while you are breathing, you're not completely filling your lungs with air
5. Exhale slowly through your mouth to the count of 8 seconds. The long slow exhale sends signals to your nervous system, telling it that you are safe, which will calm you down. Repeat this 4-8 cycle 3 times and then return your breathing to normal
6. Pay attention to your breaths – how it feels as the air it goes in, the brief pause between

inhale and exhale, cold air going in and warm air going out, your abdomen moving out and how it feels as your lungs deflate and the air is released
7. If you notice your mind wandering, which it will from time to time, gently bring it back to the breath. Every time you notice that your attention is no longer on your breath, you are training your awareness and ability to stay present
8. Try to do this daily for 10-15 minutes. If you haven't meditated before, start small and work your way up. Start with 5 minutes and add time each day until you get up to 10-15 minutes daily. Try to make meditation part of your morning routine. Like with anything, the more you do it, the more it becomes a habit

This type of meditation also trains you to be more aware of how you are breathing, which is key to controlling your heart rate and stress level.

Like going to the gym, you won't see much change day to day (although I do find that focusing on breathing for 15 minutes is very relaxing) but the long-term benefits are proven. As part of a study at Harvard University, people who practiced meditation every day for 8 weeks underwent a brain scan. The results of the study showed that there were positive changes in the areas of the brain which controls learning, memory, and emotional regulation.

Focus

> *"Through greater awareness, we can get better at keeping the mind still and quiet, so we can be more in touch with our present reality"*
> **- Ryan Holiday, from this book "Stillness Is The Key"**

Another aspect of your performance that greater awareness or mindfulness will improve is your focus. Without awareness, you don't know when your focus is no longer on a task. It's like having a conversation with someone but not really paying attention to what they are saying, you're there physically, but not mentally. In golf, "the task" is your performance process. During each phase of it, you'll need to be aware of what you are focusing on and whether it's on what you intend. Awareness tells you when you've lost focus, so you can redirect it and keep in on your task for longer.

Positive Psychology

> *"A pessimist sees the difficulty in every opportunity; an optimist sees the opportunity in every difficulty."*
> **– Winston Churchill**

Pessimism

One thing that is certain is that being negative will never help you perform well. In fact, negative thinking is a lot more powerful than positive thinking (neuroscientists say you need 3 positive thoughts to counter 1 negative).

Many golfers can fall into negative thinking patterns after a few bad shots or when they're not playing well. They struggle to see it turning around and think that more poor shots will follow. As we discussed earlier in the module, if you are unaware, and allow negative thinking (and negative self talk) to continue, it will lead to a bad mood and pessimism about the future. Because of this attitude, more negative experiences are likely to happen to you and it's unlikely that you will handle them well. An example would be having a poor driving range session before a round. A pessimist or negative thinker would begin to worry, thinking that; *"...if this continues it's going to be a bad round..."*.

Another example would be a run of poorly played holes. The pessimist will say something like, *"I'm on a bogey train and I can't get off"*, and they struggle to bounce back. An optimist on the other hand, sees an undesirable situation as something temporary (and a learning opportunity) and for this reason, something good is around the corner.

Optimism

"Optimism is at the center of mental toughness".
– **Performance Psychologist,
Dr. Michael Gervais**

In his book, "Learned Optimism", Martin Seligman, considered to be the "The Father of Positive Psychology", says that optimists achieve more, have better overall health, and have a more enjoyable life. Because they deal with challenges and setbacks better, they have lower levels of the stress hormone Cortisol, which (if persistently high) can lead to health issues, anxiety, and depression. Although some people are naturally more optimistic, research by Martin Seligman (and many others) conclude that optimism is a trainable skill that we can improve daily.

So how do we become more optimistic? Does simply telling yourself that the "glass is half full" or that you *will* shoot a good score actually work? Unfortunately, it's not that simple.

The reason that optimism is at the center of mental toughness (as Gervais says), is because it's an attitude about how you handle failure and setbacks. In other words, when things don't go your way, do you have the attitude that you can make things better, or do you get stuck in a negative mind?

There are two types of optimism: realistic and unrealistic or "self-deceptive" optimism. Realistic optimism is good, but unrealistic optimism will hold you back.

Take goal setting for example; aiming high at the beginning of the year might be considered "positive" or "optimistic", but if it's unrealistic it will only make you feel like you are falling short all the time and lead to frustration and lower your motivation and effort.

Telling yourself: *"I'm going to shoot level par today"*, when you've never broken 80 before will probably have a negative effect.

During a round, trying to be "positive" when you're not playing well, might not help. E.g., Telling yourself that: *"You are a great player"*, can sound like you are trying to convince yourself of something that isn't true, and cause you to get even more frustrated and negative. In fact, a lot of "positive thinking" falls into this category i.e., you try to convince yourself that if you think it, you *will* achieve it.

Realistic optimism is believing that if you stay present and control what you can control (commit to your process), then it's possible that things *can* go your way i.e. "If I do this (action), then it's *possible* that things can go your way (outcome)", implying that through their process (of learning and taking action), better outcomes lie ahead. This attitude further increases motivation and effort and can reduce Pervasive Fear caused from ongoing focus on what could go wrong.

Additionally, a realistic optimist achieves more because they know when things are going badly, they are still learning, and they can use experience and knowledge to adapt and improve, i.e. they have a Growth Mindset - failure and mistakes (although uncomfortable) provide us with the answers we need for future growth. As Ryan Holiday author of "The Obstacle is The Way" says:

"When you have a goal, obstacles are actually teaching you how to get where you want to go- carving you a path."

The unrealistic optimist or what we might consider a "positive thinker", can sometimes ignore what is true, downplay mistakes and the value of "process", in favor of focusing on a positive outcome i.e. "I *will* do this (outcome)" or "This *will* happen (outcome)". In this respect, positive thinking and having expectations are quite similar.

Being less "positive" and more of a realistic optimist, is what Mental Coach, Trevor Moawad calls "Neutral Thinking". A neutral thinker isn't negative or positive, instead they are always viewing their experiences non-judgmentally and the knowledge gained helps them make better decisions on what to do next. By bringing your attention to what you can do NOW, rather than focusing on positive or negative outcomes, you make positive outcomes more possible. Moawad says: *"What happens next will be determined by what you do next, not by what has happened."*

I like this approach a lot. Instead of indulging in the fantasy of "positive thinking", (which can feel fake and lead to expectations) you base your thinking on facts and the process needed for good performance. I.e., If I do these things, then it's possible that I will achieve great things!

Gratitude

"Gratitude is not only the greatest of virtues, but the parent of all the others."

– Cicero

Whereas optimism is forward looking (about the future), gratitude is about appreciating what you have *now*. Both are powerful mindsets that we *choose*. Whatever is happening in a round of golf, there is something to be grateful for. By focusing on what you are grateful for, you trigger the release of feel-good chemicals such as Serotonin, Dopamine and Oxytocin.

Let's put the game of golf in perspective. For most of us that play golf, it is a game that we *choose* to do for fun. Whatever score you shoot, you are still playing a game. You are invariably in a beautiful setting; you are healthy enough to play and you are together with friends.

Life could always be far worse than playing the game you love. You could have health problems, not be in a financial position to play or live in a place with no access to golf courses. This doesn't mean that you casually stroll around the course without the intention to perform well - I know you are a competitor, and you care about how you play - but if you find yourself focusing on the negatives, remind yourself of where you are and what you are doing. Feel the weather, look at the sky, the trees, the birds and feel the grass beneath your feet.

Exercises to become more Optimistic and Grateful
1. *At the end of each day, write down 3 times that you experienced joy in the day. This could be something small such as your morning coffee, a random act of kindness from a stranger or the sunshine on your walk to work*
2. *After a round or practice session, write down all the positive outcomes and the process you went through to achieve them (Think about all your good shots and what process led to them)*

3. What obstacles did you encounter and what did you learn to make you better?

With repetition of these exercises, you'll develop more of an optimistic and grateful attitude which will help you navigate challenges on and off the course. You'll find that you will begin to (automatically) search for solutions and possibilities, instead of focusing on the negatives.

Reducing "In The Moment" Fear

How in control are you of your thoughts, feelings and physiology in the moment? Let's find out.

Controlling Arousal

The feelings you have when you are experiencing fear is your nervous system becoming activated or "aroused". In The Moment Fear starts with feeling "nervous" or "aroused".

"Arousal Level" becomes elevated because of a situation that the brain detects as a potential threat. Upon detection of the threat, the brain's "Limbic System" activates the "Sympathetic Nervous System" to prepare us for action, and the emotion that we know as "fear" is felt. Heightened arousal (nerves) can come from either our environment or our thoughts, i.e., thinking about something you are afraid of can trigger it.

The rise in Arousal Level is proportional to how dangerous the brain perceives the threat to be and how well you can control it. It can range from light "butterflies" to a full-on panic attack.

As we discussed earlier, for our early human ancestors, threats would have been mostly physical danger, like getting eaten by a large predator. In today's world, the threats we feel are more likely to be social or from the possibility of failure. Regardless of the type of danger, the brain's response to it is the same.

Let's take a look at how a rise in arousal level helps us when we encounter serious danger. Imagine that you are hiking through woods and a Grizzly Bear comes out onto the path. Upon sight of the bear, your instinct would quickly tell you that this is a serious threat to your life (you've been conditioned throughout your life to know that this situation means danger). This would happen without you having to think about it; i.e., heightened arousal is a subconscious (automatic) response.

In this moment, your heart would immediately start beating faster to pump blood to your muscles, your muscles would tense up, and the stress hormones Adrenaline and Cortisol would start pumping into your system. Cognitive function (thinking and reasoning) becomes limited to reduce your options to either fighting or running away. This type of high arousal caused by a situation we've been conditioned to deem a threat is also called the "Fight or Flight" response, which you've probably heard of.

The game of golf is by no means life or death, but what we perceive to be a threat isn't limited to physical danger. If your hands have ever shaken while putting the ball on the tee for your first tee shot, or you've felt nervous over a 3-foot putt, then you've felt a high arousal level.

The Positive Side of Fear
On the face of it, arousal might seem as if it would hold you back from a good performance. A surge of Adrenaline, loss of cognitive ability and tension in your muscles is not going to help you make a 5ft putt to win a tournament. Golf isn't like football or other high-intensity sports where aggression can be an advantage. For golf, and anything else requiring clear thinking and fine motor skills, high arousal levels won't help.

However, there is a positive side to arousal. At low to moderate levels of it (also called "eustress"), your senses are heightened, and intensity and focus are raised. In this range of arousal, a player will typically find improvement in their performance. In fact, the research shows that there must be an increase in arousal before getting into "Flow".

But with too much arousal, also called "distress", your performance will suffer. To illustrate this, take a look at the graph which plots arousal level against performance:

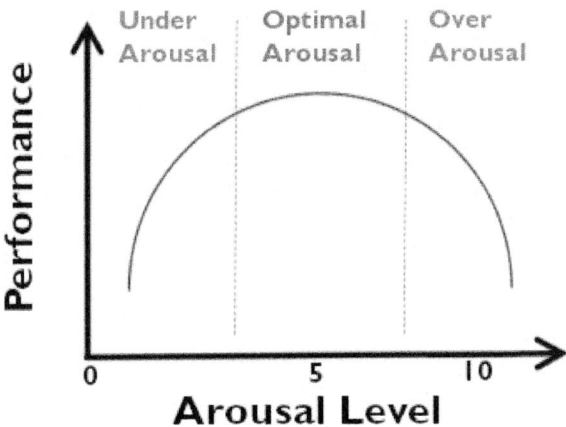

Studies show that optimal performance typically happens in the 3-7 out of 10 range, where 1 is very low arousal and 10 is very high. Being aware of where you are and being able to control it, is a key part of high performance. So how do we actively control arousal and keep it in this range?

Performing well when the pressure is on requires being aware of and controlling your level of arousal. It's also worth mentioning that when we speak about controlling arousal, it's not only about being able to decrease it. I've worked with plenty of players over the years who find that their optimal level of arousal is higher, meaning that they play better with a higher heart rate and intensity. We'll discuss this in Module 5. But let's start with what most of us need help with, which is decreasing arousal level. We can decrease arousal level by using the following techniques which activate the "Parasympathetic Nervous System".

Accept that nerves are part of The Process

"I kept telling myself, even this morning, to enjoy this moment. Enjoy the pressure. Enjoy the stress. Enjoy being uncomfortable. And don't shy away from it, embrace it… And that's what I really tried to do, is embrace that pressure all day. And I think that helped me stay a little more calm."
– Gary Woodland, after winning the US Open in 2019

Although it might be uncomfortable, butterflies and an increased heart rate is part of reaching higher levels of performance, so you might as well expect it and accept it, and not resist it. If you are nervous, you're doing something right, not wrong. By embracing it, it gives you the ability to manage it better.

It's a myth that you *need* to be calm under pressure to play well. In the summer of 2021, the PGA Tour partnered with the biofeedback device "Whoop", to add a new dimension of being able to see the player's heart rates in real time during a tournament. During Rory's win at the Wells Fargo Championship in 2021 the "Whoop Live" data showed his heart rate reached a staggering 140 beats per minute as he played the final hole. Bear in mind the average resting heart rate is 70 bpm. No doubt Rory would have preferred his heart rate to be lower, but even with an arousal level which is technically in the "fight or flight" range, he was able to make his par and secure the win. And he's someone who is used to playing under the highest pressure. Fact is, it's normal not to be calm when you are in contention or getting closer to one of your goals, so like Gary Woodland said, enjoy it and embrace it.

Accept Your Thoughts and Feelings

Whatever you are thinking and feeling at any moment in time, is always acceptable and *never* wrong. When you are aware of what is and you can accept it, you are no longer in a reactive state and trying to change it to what you think it "should be". Instead, you are in a responsive state, which gives you the power to choose what happens next.

One thing that golfers speak to me about is trying not to think negatively.

Imagine you are in a tournament, and you are about to play a tight tee shot with water down one side of the hole. Many golfers will let the thought of "*don't hit it in the water*" affect them. If that thought does occur to you, it's acceptable. Elite players can have exactly the same thoughts enter their heads. It's the resistance of these thoughts and telling yourself *not* to think about the water that makes that thought bigger, which causes tension and further increases arousal level.

Thoughts are just thoughts and have no power or meaning unless we choose to give them so.

A better approach is to accept your thoughts about the hazard and then without judgment, gently bring yourself back to what's most important – the present moment, the target, your intended shot shape, etc. With less trying *not* to do something and more acceptance of your thoughts and feelings, it will be easier to stay focused on your process.

This is an important part of the Post Shot Routine. If you can acknowledge and accept how you feel immediately after hitting a shot that you are disappointed with, it will pass quickly. I.e., It's ok to feel angry or disappointed. These primary feelings are not controllable but noticing them means you are in the present and aware of them, not reacting to them and making it worse. By doing so, you can avoid the negative interpretation and mood change that can follow, if you are unaware.

Breathe!

"When I learned how to breathe, I learned how to win"

– Tom Watson

In the moments where you feel your arousal level increasing, breathing is one of your best tools for calming the body down and getting control of your thoughts and emotions. The pathway back to safety is the breath.

When we are in the beginning of the fight or flight response, our breathing becomes shallow (in the chest), quick and erratic, meaning there's less oxygen going to the brain and hence thinking and focus becomes harder. The more we do fast chest breathing, the more we activate the fight or flight response.

Practice Good Breathing

To fully utilize the power of the breath, we need to learn how to do it properly and practice it, so it becomes our default under pressure. Basic chest breathing, that most people do throughout the day, only uses the upper part of the lungs and the inhale is usually through the mouth. The mouth was not designed by nature to breathe. Research shows that breathing in through the nose increases Oxygen uptake by 10-20%, which improves overall lung volumes[2] and stimulates the Vagus nerve (which is an integral part of the Parasympathetic nervous system, controlling such functions as heart rate). Diaphragmatic or abdominal breathing also helps deliver nutrients and eliminate waste from the heart[3].

Spend some time practicing deep belly (diaphragmatic), nasal breathing. Sit with your back upright and shoulders back as good breathing is facilitated by good posture. On your inhales, feel your belly go out as your diaphragm contracts and your lungs fill with air. The following breathing techniques are for you to experiment with and to use when you need on the course.

Breathing Techniques
"The mind is a kite, and the breath is the string."
- Mark Divine, former Navy Seal and host of "The Unbeatable Mind" podcast.

Brian MacKenzie, a Human Performance Specialist, suggests that to find your most effective breathing

---

[2] The health benefits of nose breathing, Nursing in General Practice, Ruth Allen
[3] The FlowCode, The Complete Roadmap To Flow Personality

technique to control arousal, requires experimentation. People can have a different Carbon Dioxide tolerance (its CO2 levels in your body that causes you to breath), anxiety level and physiology, so there's no "best" breathing technique for all people. Different breathing techniques can also fit different situations to maximize performance depending on what stage of it you are in.

The pattern of your breathing is important. When I ask new students what breathing techniques they use, they will often tell me that they just take a deep breath if they feel nervous. Although this is better than nothing, it's the repetition and pattern of the breath that helps lower arousal as much as the increase in oxygen.

There are hundreds of different breathing techniques which vary the time for inhale, hold and exhale. Explore these different breathing techniques (do 10 sets of each) and pay attention to how it changes your mental and physical state. If your watch has a heart rate monitor, you can check your heart rate as you do the exercises and see which technique is most effective in lowering it. The ratios refer to the length of inhale-hold-exhale-hold in seconds.

1. Start with "Box Breathing", which is 1-1-1-1 ratio e.g., inhale through your nose to the count of 4, hold for a count of 4, exhale through your nose or mouth to the count of 4, and hold for 4, then repeat. Try changing the counts to 2 seconds, 3 seconds, or 5 seconds

2. Try a 1-1-2-1 technique, which for example would be 4 seconds for the inhale, 4 seconds for the hold, 8 second exhale and 4 second hold
3. Try a 1-2-2 technique, which would be a 6 second inhale, 12 second hold and a 12 second exhale (this one is more difficult)
4. Try the 4-7-8 technique, which is a 4 second inhale, 7 second hold and 8 second exhale

After practicing these different techniques, you'll know what is most effective for you to use when you need it on the course.

Use Your Eyes

What might surprise you is that our eyes are not only for seeing shapes and colors, but they are also directly connected to the nervous system and hence, are another controller of arousal level. Dr. Andrew Huberman, a professor of neuroscience at the Stanford University School of Medicine, has studied the link between vision and the limbic system. He says, *"Vision and our visual system, is perhaps the strongest lever by which we can shift our state of mind and body."*

When we are relaxed, our vision is wider or "panoramic". When we are stressed or excited, our field of vision is narrowed.

Just like breathing, which we can use to change our inner state, changing our vision is also bi-directional i.e., arousal level change changes vision, but consciously changing our field of vision changes arousal level. This is why looking at a computer or our mobile phone for hours can make us stressed, whereas a walk in nature with beautiful views can be relaxing – it opens up our field of vision.

To decrease arousal level, widen your field of vision and take in as much of your environment as you can. Try to see everything without focusing on anything specific. Most golf courses have beautiful scenery, so to do this in between shots should be easy and will have a calming effect.

Reframing Nerves

Heightened arousal is also experienced when you feel emotional states other than fear. Excitement and joy can also trigger it. For this reason, arousal level can be controlled simply by interpreting it differently. This technique is based on the fact that physiologically, anxiety and excitement are the same, but mentally they are very different. Excitement is a better mindset as it's about optimism and positive possibilities, compared to an anxious mind which is focused on what could go wrong. Dr. Alison Woods Brooks, an assistant professor at Harvard Business School, conducted a study to see the effects of this technique. She studied groups of people who were asked to do anxiety inducing activities, such as public speaking, karaoke contests or math tests. Half the group were told to do what they could calm down and the other half were told that what they were feeling was excitement. The results showed that those who "reframed" the feeling of high arousal as excitement instead of fear, performed significantly better.

The next time you experience butterflies and an increased heart rate, choose to see it as you being excited about the good things that can happen. As we've already discussed, you know that the increased Adrenaline, sensory awareness and focus that comes with "nerves" are a positive, so that coupled with a view that it's excitement not performance anxiety will make you feel less "In The Moment Fear" and more excited and energized.

Arousal exercise:
How will you control your arousal level in your next round?

Slow Down

Another symptom of In The Moment Fear is doing things quicker. It's the fight or flight response at work to try to move you out of the uncomfortable situation. You might rush through your Pre Shot Routine and not think through the shot properly, walk faster in between shots and swing faster. When you're feeling high arousal, you will need to be aware of your "cadence" i.e., how fast you are moving and walking. Tell yourself to slow down. What you perceive to be a slower pace will probably be about normal. Slow down your walk, your routine, and your swing. When you are feeling high arousal, rehearse a slower swing during your practice swings.

Justin Rose said that before the final round of the 2013 US Open (which he won) he knew his tendency would be to start rushing, so he slowed himself down as soon as he woke up, even brushing his teeth slower and eating his breakfast slower.

If you are feeling nervous, be aware of your pace and if you notice that you are rushing, slow it down. With well-practiced shot routines, you will be able to take a similar time for each shot, no matter what shot it is in the round.

Visualization To Change Internal State

> *"I pretended that I was playing each shot at my home course against my friends."*
> **– Sophia Popov after the final round of her 2020 Women's British Open win**

Visualization is not only helpful in telling the body what to do before you hit a shot, but research in the field of neuroscience also supports visualization as being a way to improve mood and change how you feel.

Simply put, visualization is creating images or movies in your mind. Some students will tell me that they *"can't visualize"*, but if you can close your eyes and imagine what you had for breakfast this morning, then you *can* visualize.

Imagining something happy can make you feel happy. Imagining something relaxing can help you feel more relaxed. Imagining something with high energy can give you more energy, and so on. In our imagination lies the opportunity to adjust our mental, emotional and physical state at any stage of a round. If you are feeling anxious or under pressure, going to a "happy place" in your mind is a good technique for staying calm and in a good mood. Simply focusing on something (or someone) that you love, or happy memories can release "feel-good" chemicals and reduce stress.

What you decide to visualize is a personal preference, but it could be a favorite vacation spot, walking along a sandy beach, being with friends or family, or like Sophia Popov, visualizing playing with friends during the final round of a major.

Jordan Spieth says that if he needs a boost of confidence, he will imagine some of his best performances, via his "personal high-light reel".

Some players will keep photos of their families on their bags, which they can look at to create a feeling of happiness and gratitude.

Visualization Exercise:
Write down 3 things that you can visualize in the pressure moments to reduce feelings of fear and make you feel more confident and secure.

Self Talk

> *"Language is the most powerful drug known to mankind"*
>
> **– Rudyard Kipling**

Another trigger, or way to control our internal state and reduce In The Moment Fear, is self talk. How we talk to ourselves is a big factor in our confidence level, self-belief, motivation, and ability to deal with challenges and setbacks. The best coach you have is the one within you and the most powerful voice you hear is your own. It's time to think carefully about how you use it.

In the pressure moments, there can be a lot of noise or "chatter" in your head and self talk is an effective way to direct your attention away from it and stay mentally strong. It's also a way to "prime" your subconscious and increase self-belief.

First, let's distinguish between thoughts and self talk. As we've discussed before, most thoughts occur subconsciously, without our control and many are what would be considered "negative". Self talk on the other hand, is something that we *choose* and is *fully within our control*. Much of what we consider negative self talk is actually negative thoughts which appear as a reaction to undesirable outcomes and/or uncomfortable feelings. It's one thing to have a negative thought caused by an outcome, but you can choose what you say to yourself afterwards and this takes practice.

In this lesson, I'd like to show you how to make your self talk more proactive and to help use it as a tool to control your internal state and enhance your performance. The skill of self talk comes in finding the right thing to say to yourself daily and in the pressure moments. Not all self talk works for all people in all situations. To do this well it requires reflection, intention, and practice.

What story do you tell yourself every day?

What we say to ourselves throughout our days and during our rounds has a big influence on how we feel, how we perform and whether we become who we want to be over time.

After his first major win, Brooks Koepka told the media that he is *"a big tournament player"*, which could have easily backfired. However, Brooks has clearly been telling himself that he's a "big tournament player" for some time and has now become that player, winning a further 3 majors within 2 years. Do you think that Brooks doesn't have doubts like the rest of us? Of course he does. But he doesn't allow himself to listen to them, and instead tells himself about the success he's going to have.

Negative Self Talk

A lot of what players call negative self talk is actually an automatic negative thought which occurs after a setback or when you are feeling frustrated or angry. Examples of negative thoughts are:

> *"That was such a bad shot."*
> *"You should have made that putt."*
> *"What a dumb decision that was!"*
> *"You suck!"*
> *"This is going to be a bad round."*
> *"Maybe you're just not cut out for this."*
> *"Why does bad luck always happen to me?"*
> *"You've lost your swing."*
> *"You're in a slump."*

Steps To Better Self Talk

1. **Self-awareness**

As with most of the training in this book, the first step to having better self talk is with awareness. The more aware you are of what you are feeling and thinking, the more agile and selective you can be with your responses. As we've already discussed, most of our negative thoughts are just noise and the brain doing its job of highlighting possible threats, they are certainly not worth verbalizing (either in your mind or out loud). By being present to how you feel and what you are placing our attention on as the events of our rounds unfold, you can do a better job of accepting and not reacting with negative self talk.

2. **Decide on Better Self Talk**

Self talk is more effective when it's decided upon before you use it. Let's start by taking a look at some of the different types of self talk which have different uses for different situations you could be in on the course or practice. After this module, you'll have a selection of personalized self talk scripts which you can use to navigate any situation.

Positive Self Talk

"It's the repetition of affirmations that leads to belief. And once that belief becomes a deep conviction, things begin to happen."

- Muhammad Ali

As with what you visualize for your future, the stories you tell yourself each day will have a big influence on what becomes of your life. If you continually *choose* to tell yourself about your great qualities and what you are capable of doing, you increase your chances of doing it. That said, positive self talk will only work if you believe it. A player who is lacking confidence or self esteem will feel worse if they try to convince themselves how good they are using positive self talk.

Positive self talk should speak to your qualities and values, not specific events or outcomes. As you create these "Self Talk Scripts", think about what gives you the right to say these things to yourself. These positive affirmations can be used daily or as part of your pre round warm up or in between shots. Examples of this would be:

"What a great shot! That's what I am capable of doing."

"I have a world class short game".

"I've got this shot."

"I am mentally tough and can overcome any setback or challenge."

"I am relentless. I keep pushing hard every day to get better."

"Nobody will outwork me."

"I always give 100% and never give up."

"I have the qualities of a champion."

"I love pressure."

"I am confident in my ability."

"The challenge of competition raises my focus and my game."

"I am a consistent and powerful driver."

"I love this game and I love the pressure."

You can also use self talk to redirect yourself to your Player Identity, such as: *"Confidence, Commitment, Class and Persistence"*, those values you will uphold in every practice session and round.

It doesn't need to be before and during your rounds that you use positive affirmations – make it part of your daily morning routine to tell yourself how great you are!

Action Based or Neutral Self Talk

"I just told myself to focus and lock in -- that's what I told myself all day. I really did a good job of staying present and focusing as hard as I could on every shot. That's what golf is -- not getting ahead of yourself and just locking in and giving every shot your full attention."

– Patrick Cantlay after winning the BMW Championship in 2021

Sometimes, "being positive" doesn't work or isn't required. You might be better off using "action based", or "neutral" self talk which can bring your attention to simple actions you can take during each phase of the round i.e., your "Process". Examples are:

"Commit to the shot." (In the Pre Shot Routine)
"One shot at a time." (When thinking ahead)
"Be present…" (At any time)
"Target, Align, Commit and Accept." (During the Shot Routine)

"What do you feel right now?" (In between shots)
"Let it go and move on." (In the Post Shot Routine)
"Breathe, relax and slow down." (In between shots)
"Walk tall and be confident." (In between shots)
"Light grip pressure and focus on the back of the ball." (In the Pre Shot Routine)

Motivational Self Talk

If you find that you need to push yourself or raise your intensity level, you will benefit from motivational self talk. As we discussed in the Post Shot Routine section, the tone of it can slightly firmer if you feel like that works better for you.

Some examples are:
"Let's go!"
"You can do this."
"You can turn this around."
"You can do better!"
"Good thing you are a great scrambler!"
"The next shot can be a great shot."
"This is a great opportunity for you to show your recovery skills."
"Fight for every shot until the final putt drops on 18."
"Play this next shot as if it's the last one you will ever hit."
"You love the conditions being tough like this. Bring it on!"
"Nothing can affect your confidence!"

"I" vs "You" in Self Talk

Studies that have been done on self talk indicate that the use of the "I", "You" and your name, can make a difference in the effectiveness of it.

A study published in the Journal of Personality and Social Psychology found that when people used the "You" or your name form when using self talk, they performed better under stress than people who used the "I" form. The conclusion is that when people think of themselves as another (or "second") person, they create mental distance from what they are doing (or about to do). They feel less anxiety and are able to be more objective, as it's less personal. Also, when you receive instructions on how to do something, you are told in the "you" or your name form. The "you" form is like your coach or teacher talking to you and guiding you.

On the other hand, the "I" form is probably more effective for positive affirmations.

Step 3: Practice Better Self Talk

In your Golf State of Mind notebook, do the following exercise:

1. Write down some situations that you believe self talk would be helpful to you. E.g., To start your day, before your round, on the first tee, during your Pre Shot Routine, after a poor shot or bad hole, etc.
2. What negative thoughts do you sometimes have and how can you respond to them? Think

about some of the things you've said to yourself when you've been successful in the past. Write these possible situations out and practice your response to them with your self talk. Remember that you need to be able to validate positive self talk and believe it, otherwise "neutral" or process based self talk is better

At the end of this exercise, you will have a list of self talk scripts which can be used to build confidence and navigate the challenges of a round of golf. Reflect on your use of self talk at the end of your rounds (you'll see it on the Post Round Review template, which we'll discuss in module 6).

Body Language

When most people think of "body language", they think of how they look to others. Although this is something to be considered, your body language is actually another "controller" of your internal state.

Research shows that body language and facial expressions influence our brain chemistry and hormone levels which can make us feel different.

When we adopt strong, confident postures (shoulders back, chest out, eyes up), we not only show others that we are feeling confident, but we change our emotional state. By adopting a confident posture, we feel more confident. And by feeling more confident, we get into better thinking patterns. Good posture tricks our brains into producing feel-good chemicals called endorphins. Contrarily, when we are in weaker postures, we tell others and ourselves that we are feeling weak. Our brains trigger the production of Cortisol, also known as the "stress hormone".

If this is true, then those times when you can tell that someone is playing poorly by their body language – when their head has dropped and they are looking down with hunched shoulders, they are weakening their chances of turning it around. They're bringing more negative energy towards themselves.

Author James Clear tells us that a study was done between Harvard and Columbia Universities which had 42 people adopt different body postures, and afterwards, their hormone levels were tested.

The results showed that those with the more "high-power" postures (standing up, back straight, shoulders back), had higher levels of testosterone and lower levels of cortisol i.e., those people felt more confident, powerful, and less stressed. Conversely, those people that adopted weak postures like being slumped over, having hunched shoulders, looking down etc.), had higher levels of Cortisol, lower levels of Testosterone and they felt less confident.

The same thing works for facial expressions. Actors use facial expressions to create feelings within themselves and make a performance more authentic. E.g., Frowning can make you feel concerned and worried by itself. Smiling can immediately lighten your mood and make you feel happier. This is where the expression, "put on your game face" comes from. If you look as if you are confident, focused and determined and it sends messages to the brain to say that you are. What do your facial expressions say about how you want to feel on the golf course?

Use body language and facial expressions to control your internal state. Think of the top players in the men and women's games and you'll be able to see their confident demeanor and posture as they walk the fairways. It's a trained part of their player persona which helps them feel more confident, no matter how they are playing.

Make it part of your performance process and plan for your round to walk and look the way you want to feel.

Body Language Exercise:
What body language and facial expressions will you choose to have in your next round?

The Alter Ego Effect

Another way that we can use imagination, self talk and body language to achieve our best mental, emotional, and physical state is through developing an "Alter Ego" or "Player Persona".

In Module 1 we talked about the values that you want to bring to every practice session and round and creating a Player Identity or "motto" which speaks to those values. An Alter Ego can give you access to those values and characteristics whenever you choose.

In his book, "The Alter Ego Effect", Todd Herman describes how helping his clients find their "Alter Ego" allows them to be the best version of themselves in whatever it is they are doing. So, what is an "Alter Ego", and how can it help you play better golf? Let's take a look.

What is an "Alter Ego"?
We all play different roles in our lives, which require us to access different sides of ourselves. E.g., You might be one way with your family, one way at work and another way when you're on the golf course. With your family, you might be fun and loving, and on the golf course, you might be more serious, focused and competitive. Being the loving, family person on the course probably won't help you play your best golf.

Todd Herman tells us that the Alter Ego Effect is about identifying the role that we want to play and creating an embodiment or personification of it i.e., your "Alter Ego", which we can then use as a vehicle or gateway to bring out those qualities when we are performing.

E.g., if you were to give a speech, would you rather be timid, fearful, and looking down at the ground with your shoulders hunched? Or would you want to be confident, authoritative, have good posture, smile and have eye contact with the audience? Obviously, you would want to be in the role of the latter, as that would be more conducive to a better and more successful speech. If you went in there with someone or something in your mind that embodies those qualities, it can help you activate those qualities within you. An example would be a "high energy, enthusiastic and exciting Tony Robbins".

"Act as if" to make you feel like you are
Another way to think about the Alter Ego effect, would be a junior golfer imagining themselves as one of their idols while playing. If you played junior golf, I'm sure you did this. By pretending you are a golfer that embodies those qualities of a champion, you can activate those same qualities from within you. But let's not be naive, acting as if you are Brooks Koepka or Lydia Ko, isn't going to give you their technical skills. Neither will having the Alter Ego of Tony Robbins turn into one of the best motivational speakers. The Alter Ego effect is not about "faking it till you make it" and pretending that you have skills that you don't, it's about changing the way you feel inside. By "acting as if" you are your Alter Ego, you can "feel like you are", which can allow you to access your best skills with less inhibition and deal with challenges better.

Actors do this all the time. By using their imagination, body language and facial expressions, they can create the authentic feelings felt by the character that they are portraying. By getting into the character/role of your powerful Alter Ego, you can do the same.

To do this, you will need to explore your Alter Ego in detail and think about how they would behave in different situations, what their attitudes and beliefs are, and what makes them great. E.g., how would Tiger Woods handle a bad shot or double bogey?

Detaching you as a player from you as a person
Having an Alter Ego to maximize performance is not a new concept, especially in sports. Soccer player Zlatan Ibrahimovic "becomes" a Lion. Kobe Bryant became "The Black Mamba". Many boxers become their Alter Ego in the ring. Sugar Ray Leonard once said that if "Ray Leonard" showed up for the fight he would lose, but "Sugar Ray Leonard" was invincible, as if they were two different people. I believe that having a separate persona for yourself as an athlete or player can explain why the top sports men and women, such as Ibrahimovic, Roger Federer and Serena Williams, have had such long and successful careers. Whatever is going on in their personal lives doesn't matter as they are able to flip a switch to become their Alter Ego or best performing self, which allows them to perform consistently at the highest level.

Additionally, when you detach your performer self from your actual self, it means you are less self-conscious and don't take your performance as personally. Because you are a performer when you are on the course, not your everyday self, you eliminate a lot of the doubt and fear that your everyday self might feel before and during a round.

Finding your Alter Ego
Think about who you are when you play your best golf? What characteristics and attributes do you have? Who is the player that you want to be in practice and on the golf course?

You can go back to your values list or player philosophy to help you with this e.g., they are confident, focused, tough, excited, positive, optimistic, fun, have strong body language, etc.

Next, find an Alter Ego which embodies those qualities. Some examples are:

- A model player or sports person e.g., Collin Morikawa, Tiger Woods, Lexi Thompson, Michael Jordan or Lebron James
- An animal that embodies the strengths you would like to have on the golf course e.g. A lion, snake, bulldog, hawk, etc.
- A fictional character
- A combination of words and that person/animal e.g. *"I'm a mentally tough Rory McIlroy, Mentally Tough like Brooks, or a "Powerful Aggressive Lion"*

Activating Your Alter Ego

Once you have defined your Alter Ego and who or what that is, we need to activate it. You can also think of this as "putting your game face on". Like with the NLP triggers, you need an action to transition into your Alter Ego, like Clark Kent would go into the telephone booth to become Superman. Todd Herman tells us that it works best when it's a physical action, such as putting on your cap, your shirt, your golf shoes or glove.

Make it part of your pre round ritual to activate your Alter Ego and get into the role. By doing this, you'll be able to create a performance state more conducive to confidence, freedom, and success.

Anchors and Triggers

Have you ever noticed that when you hear a certain song or catch a whiff of a smell, that it can make you feel a certain way before you remember what memory is being triggered? Through your "Associate Memory", your mind has been "programmed" to associate certain feelings with certain memories. People are often nostalgic about certain happy times in their lives and use things like music and clothes to recreate how they felt back then.

Memories (and their subsequent feelings) are triggered mostly through our senses, by something we see, feel, hear, smell or taste. Because the connection happens quickly, the sensations themselves can "tap into our subconscious" and make us feel a certain way before we are consciously aware of why.

"Anchors" are what connect us to those previously experienced internal states and feelings of the past, like the music I mentioned above. Anchors can be verbal (words), auditory (sound), or kinesthetic (touch).

Although most of this programming of the mind and subsequent triggering happens organically throughout our lives, without us thinking about doing it, we can use a process called "Anchoring" to strengthen the links between the conscious and subconscious minds. In other words, we can store positive memories more deeply and trigger the internal state associated with them.

If you've heard of "NLP" or "Neurolinguistic Programming", this is essentially what it is.

The Global NLP Institute says:

"Anchoring is a process where a specific stimulus (cue, trigger) is connected to a memory recall, state or state change, or another response. Anchoring occurs naturally all the time. You likely have several powerful anchors in place; a certain smell may remind you of a specific person (perfume, etc.). Each time you see something, it can bring you back to the state or a past memory (a photograph, a living room etc.). The same occurs when you hear a certain sound or piece of music."

Memory/Internal State <-> Anchor/Trigger <-> Stimulus

Anchoring

To start the anchoring process, decide what positive internal states you are going to anchor, and recall the times you've felt them in the past. E.g., Confidence, Focus, Happiness, Calmness, etc. These will probably be memories of some of your best rounds or shots, or times where you have successfully overcome challenges. Let's take the example of improving your confidence in your short game.

1. Firstly, think of some of your best ever short game shots. If you have been keeping a "shot

log" in your Performance Journal, you will find some there
2. Like with visualization, the Anchoring process is best done after meditating for 10-15 mins
3. Try to remember each shot vividly – the golf course, the greens, the shot you had, the look and feel of the shot, who you were playing with, the sounds, colors, etc.
4. Remember exactly how you felt in those moments before, during and after those shots. At the moment you feel that internal state again, you "fire" the anchor. I.e., you say your word, make your touch or sound or look at a visual trigger
5. With repetition of this process, this anchor can be a "trigger" or "cue" of that internal state which you can use in your Pre Shot Routine (or as needed during your rounds)

Types of Anchors

Experiment with the following anchors and see what works best for you in triggering that internal state. Different people can respond differently to different sensory cues i.e., some people are more verbal, some more kinesthetic, etc. The more you use an anchor, the more effective it will be at triggering the desired internal state.

Verbal Anchors/Cues

When you take yourself back to your positive memory/internal state, think about a word that best describes how you felt at that time. Examples are:

"Easy"
"Committed"
"Strong"
"Smooth"
"Powerful"
"Focused"
"Dominant"
"Love"

Once you've picked your word, "fire" it during your visualization and then use it in your Pre Shot Routine.

Visual Triggers:

Visualization itself is a trigger of an internal state, e.g., imagining walking down a sandy beach can make you feel relaxed, as if you've done it before, that is most likely how you felt and hence that same state is triggered.

Add that some players might have a photo of their family on their bag.

Colors can be powerful triggers. Advertisers carefully choose colors as they are emotional triggers and can change the way you feel about a brand or an experience.

Is there a color that you would associate with your positive experiences? When you reflect and find a memory that matches a desired internal state, try to give that a color.

Louis Oosthuizen used a red dot on his glove to trigger a more focused mental state during his Pre Shot Routine on his way to winning the 2010 Open Championship.

Tiger wears red on Sunday because that color means dominance and gives him power.

Auditory Cues
Here are some examples of using sound as an anchor:
- Playing music while you are visualizing you at your best and then playing the same music before your round and in your mind during the round
- Snap the Velcro on your glove
- Say a word out loud

Kinesthetic Triggers
Here are some examples of ways to use touch as an anchor:
- Tapping yourself
- Press your thumb and index finger together
- Rickie Fowler touches his cap as part of his Pre Shot Routine
- Tiger Woods blinks methodically
- Fred Couples tugs his shirt

It doesn't only have to be when you are visualizing that you can do the anchoring process. Immediately after a good shot or whenever you are experiencing your optimal internal state you can do it. E.g., If you hit a great drive and your anchor is the word "Commitment", then you would say that word at that time. The word "Commitment" can then be used as a trigger of confidence in the Pre Shot Routine.

Returning To The Present

A key skill when you are under pressure, when the mind is harder to keep still, is being able to return to the present.

In fact, from my ongoing work with competitive golfers, I'd say that being in the present is one of the biggest challenges that golfers face and it's such a key factor in performance.

Being in the present is becoming more of a challenge for all of us in our today's world because we rarely allow ourselves just to "be", without the need of some sort of entertainment. Instead, for most of our waking hours we are "plugged in" to our devices and in a constant state of distraction, with social media, news and videos. Many people have become addicted to their phones (especially juniors) and find it hard to spend moments without them (the average person checks their mobile device over 50 times a day). The longer-term effects of this are:

- Diminished ability to be able to focus for longer periods and get deep into a single task, affecting productivity
- Less awareness of our thinking and feelings, so you can easily get caught up in negative thinking
- More stress and anxiety, meaning less of our energy is going towards appreciating the present moment

Whenever I speak with a student after one of their best rounds, they describe being present and focusing on "one shot at a time". If this is true, then making it a goal to be more present on and off the course will undoubtedly help performance.

When you are present, you are experiencing the moment to its fullest. You are just "being" - *not* thinking and judging. Your focus is at its sharpest, your mind at its quietist and you have direct access to your skills.

One of my Tour player clients told me about her experience of having a 1 shot lead with 3 holes to play. She had seen the leaderboard, which immediately made her feel more nervous, but we had trained her for the challenges of being in that situation.

She knew that staying in the present moment was going to help most during those long walks in between shots. She knew that her mind would want to start predicting the future and her chances of success, but if she let it, it would reduce her chances of getting the outcome she desired. She told me that those last few holes felt like hours, but she stayed patient and kept returning her mind to the present, something she had practiced daily. Time did eventually pass, and she achieved her first win on Tour.

How To Access The Present In Your Rounds
The best way to access the present at any moment in your rounds, is through your senses i.e., What you see, feel, hear and smell. As you walk the fairways:

- Shift your attention to the feel of the ground beneath your feet, the textures of the different grasses and the slopes of the terrain
- Notice the temperature and feel of the wind on your skin
- Notice the colors of the sky, the clouds, the trees moving in the wind
- Notice the many different shades of green you can see on the grass

Notice the sensations of your breath.

Do Daily Tasks "Mindfully"
When you are doing any task, tell yourself that you are going to do this, and *only* this, for the time that you've allocated to it. If you are practicing your chipping, that's what you are doing. If you are brushing your teeth, that's what you are doing. Notice if you become distracted and return to the present. With phones being the number one distraction for most of us, put your phone somewhere that you can't reach for it until after you've finished your highly focused session. By making it a goal to do every task more mindfully, you'll train yourself to be more present, get deeper into the task and get so much more out of your time.

Returning to The Present Exercise:
What are some ways that you can return to the present moment when you notice your mind wandering to unhelpful thoughts?

Practicing For Pressure

> *"Most people stay in their comfort zone. Improvement comes when we're in the Ugly Zone."*
> – **Dr. Dave Alred**

On the golf course and in tournaments:

- Every shot counts and has a consequence
- Every shot is a unique challenge
- There are several minutes between shots for possible "thinking" time
- Your heart rate or "arousal level" is higher

Although most golfers know this to be true, they spend little time practicing in a way that will help them to adapt to these changing (external and internal) conditions. Instead, they stay in their comfort zone by over-practicing the technical and not having consequences for shots. This improves the quality of their shots at the time but doesn't lead to improvement in the skills necessary to perform better on the course. They don't like being in the "Ugly Zone", and hence they spend little time doing more effective practice which might show them up or expose them to failure.

Although the golf course is the best place to practice (after all, that's where we play the game), most of us have more frequent access to driving ranges and practice facilities. For this reason, it's important to find ways to make it challenging and interesting and simulate what we experience on the golf course.

I should clarify that I'm not implying that a golfer shouldn't practice their technique – of course we need to work on technical skill development. But if you are to become a player who performs well under pressure, you'll need to allocate time in every practice session to develop your performance skills and train in "the Ugly Zone".

Performance Practice or "Training Ugly", trains you to:

- Develop a "no limits" mindset
- Adapt quickly to challenges
- Think clearly in difficult situations
- Be more comfortable being uncomfortable
- Develop a clear, transferable process
- Deal with nerves and higher arousal levels

Performance Drills

I have plenty of performance drills and ways to create a competitive environment during practice in the Golf State of Mind Practice Book.

Performance drills are about pushing yourself to beat previous personal bests and feel the pressure that it brings with it. It's called "The Ugly Zone", because it doesn't feel good to be there. But being at the margins of your current (or perceived) ability level is the only place that you are going to be able to figure out how to push forward to the next level of better.

Performance drills are enhanced by stat tracking in your rounds and scorekeeping in your practice sessions, so you know precisely the areas of the game you need to improve, and how much time to allocate. A simple example is a player that is looking to improve proximity to the hole from around the greens. They might pick 10 locations of varying difficulty (i.e., lie, carry, distance from the hole, etc.) and see how many shots they can get within 10 ft of the hole (hitting one ball only from each location). Every time they go to practice, they would do this drill (from the same locations each time) and aim to beat their best score. If their personal best is 6 out of 10, the "Ugly Zone" as Dr. Alred calls it, would start at 4 or 5.

As Dr. Dave Alred says:

> 'It's at the margin that you're always trying to improve. If a player is able to do 10 of something, we're looking to get 11 or 12. The philosophy of a no limits mentality is that you are always trying to get better than your previous self."

Possible failure, frustration and being uncomfortable are all a part of the Ugly Zone. A player must learn to stay in the fight and develop/learn mental strategies to keep their confidence and self-esteem intact and withstand the fear of failure (just like they have to when under pressure on the course). Performance Practice is a great way to practice for pressure and give us insight into the best process to focus on when we are playing, so we can access our best technical skills when it matters most.

By doing the drills and performing better at them in practice, you'll increase your confidence and your ability to execute on the course.

Using Your Imagination During Practice Sessions
Your imagination can be a great compliment to your performance practice sessions and help you create uncomfortable internal states, so you learn how to adjust and become "more comfortable being uncomfortable". Before your session, ask yourself:

- What situations make you feel uncomfortable and will likely raise your arousal level?
- What situations will you be in if you are to achieve your goals?
- What challenging shots will you face in your next round?
- What situations/scenarios would likely cause negative thinking patterns?
- What will you *do* in those situations?

Create vivid representations of them in your mind i.e., who you are playing with, the tournament, the golf course, the colors, the weather, etc.

Examples are:
- Your tee shot on the 1st hole of a tournament
- Your tee shot on the 2nd hole after a double bogey start

- Being under par at the turn and having a chance to shoot your best score
- Your tee shot on the 18th with a one-shot lead
- Having to get up and down from around the green to force a play-off or win a tournament
- Making a 2-putt from 30ft to win the tournament
- A 5-foot putt to win

For each shot:
1. Imagine a difficult scenario
2. Considering your heart rate could be 120 bpm or more during a tournament, run on the spot to get it there before hitting the shot. If you have a heart rate monitor on your watch, you can get it to the desired heart rate before playing each shot
3. Go through your full Pre Shot Routine
4. Practice your Post Shot Routine and how respond to the outcome
5. Take 1-2 minutes break in between shots to simulate the golf course and to make sure you don't get into a rhythm of hitting shots (one of the pitfalls of normal driving range practice that leads to an "illusion of competence"). You could use the time in between to do some meditation or to practice being alone with your thoughts (don't get your phone out to occupy the time)

By doing more Performance Practice, you'll discover more about the effectiveness of your current "performance process" in controlling your internal state and preparing for shots, and you can experiment with the tools covered in modules 3 and 4 to improve it. By succeeding in practice in these challenging situations you'll increase your confidence and chances of success during the real thing.

Keep Expanding Your Comfort Zone

If you are constantly stepping into unfamiliar situations in your life, it means you are growing at a rapid pace. If you are constantly seeking a comfort zone, you are stagnant. Only when you lose the fear of suffering – that no matter what happens, "this is how you will be", can you explore your life in full depth and dimension."

— **Sadhguru**

Learning how to push through fear and discomfort comes with experience. If the size of fear is proportional to the size of what we perceive we could lose, then it makes sense to gradually increase the amount we have at stake and learn how to successfully manage the thoughts, feelings and discomfort that come at each level.

E.g., If you have a fear of public speaking that you want to overcome, you wouldn't do it by speaking in front of a thousand people – that would be too overwhelming. Instead, you would gradually expand your comfort zone or "graduate pressure" by speaking in front of smaller groups and working your way up to larger ones. At each level, you can learn how to deal with the mental and physical changes that occur when fear is present, and you become more comfortable with it. As you learn how to navigate each situation, your fear begins to diminish, and your confidence increases. It's the same thing in golf – each level of the game comes with its own set of mental challenges to overcome. E.g., it would be extremely difficult to manage the thoughts and feelings that come with leading a Major Championship if you've never played in one before. Jack Nicklaus said that it took him a lot of second place finishes to learn how to win.

By expanding your comfort zone each time, what you perceive as threatening changes. The amygdala, which is the part of the brain that controls the fear response in humans, desensitizes, so what might have triggered fear in the past, no longer does. In the documentary "Free Solo" about the free solo rock climber Alex Honnold, we learn that after risking his life daily, his ability to feel fear had diminished to almost zero. Neuroscientists were shocked to learn from an MRI scan of his brain that his amygdala had shrunk to the smallest they had ever seen.

Obviously you are not risking your life by playing golf, but by putting yourself in situations that make you feel uncomfortable, and approaching it with the right mindset, your fear response will reduce to more manageable and performance enhancing levels.

"Every day do something that makes you uncomfortable."

- David Goggins

It's important to appreciate that any situation which makes you feel uncomfortable, helps you grow and develop resilience. We can't build the mental skills needed to become the best we can, by sitting on the couch. We need to be continually tested and learn how to quiet the ego and be our best performing selves in the big moments.

My goal for this module, as the title implies, is for you to play with less fear and more confidence. With a Growth Mindset and the tools to manage your inner self, I hope that you will now see pressure situations as a win-win. There is never any losing. Pressure is an opportunity to learn how to channel focus and get into flow and find out what you can do to perform even better.

One of the most fulfilling things about this game is the feeling you get from overcoming challenges and reaching new levels of better and that always involves pressure and fear. By persevering, learning and growing you will increase your skill at managing it, and you'll soon discover that there are no limits to how good you can become.

Module 5: Pre-Round Preparation and Warm-Up

"The more prepared I feel, the more entitled I feel to hit good shots"
— Adam Scott

What you do *before* a round has a big effect on how you play *during* it. Whether you are a weekend golfer with little time to practice or a full-time player, you *must* feel prepared and ready for the challenges ahead. Doubts and fears can arise if you don't have a clear plan for your Pre Round Preparation and Mental Warm Up. As with everything we've covered so far, there are many different ways you can go about this, and hence you must find what works for you.

Know The Course and Have a Strategy

Before you play, you increase your chances of playing well by getting to know the course and developing a strategy. Anticipating the challenges that each hole will bring, means that you can do a lot of the decision making *before* the round, when you don't have the emotions that can be present during it or when you're feeling under

Module 5: Pre-Round Preparation and Warm-Up

pressure. Emotions will never help decision making, information does, so we need to gather as much as possible before we play.

The 7 Point Course Strategy Preparation
1. Use the course yardage book and/or the Google Earth measuring tool to measure the width of the landing areas for each tee shot. E.g., if you hit your driver an average distance of 250 yds, find out how much room you have at that distance off the tee and decide if a shorter club (and having a slightly longer 2nd shot) is a higher percentage strategy. Remember that every shot is about determining the risk and reward of all the options and picking the shot that gets you closest to your optimal target for an acceptable level of risk. Your shot dispersion data will tell you what the probability is of landing the ball within a target area. To pick a shot, you'll want to have at least 75-80% certainty that you won't be OB, in water or unplayable (the rough is fine). In the Golf State of Mind Practice System, I can show you how to measure your shot dispersion for each club. On holes where there is water or OB on one side of the hole, the center of the fairway may not be the best target. Your target should be the center of your shot dispersion, so find a target that will fit your dispersion into the hole and reduce your probability of going in the water or OB

Good golf course designers will try to trick you into thinking there is less room for your tee and approach shots, than there actually is. By looking at the aerial views you will see the true width of the landing areas, as in the image below:

2. Anticipate 3 different pin positions on each green and think about how this could affect how you play the hole
3. For your tee shots and approaches, use the aerial view to consider the good and bad miss and mark off these areas in your yardage book. Even though you might not know the pin positions ahead of time, you should still be able to determine where you have the best chance of an up and down around the green and where it will be more difficult
4. Anticipate different situations that would allow you to go for a par 5 in two and which would mean that you would lay up. If you are going to lay up, what yardage will you lay up to?
5. What are the distances to the center or widest areas of the greens on the par 3's?
6. What is the weather forecast and predicted wind direction for your round? How could this affect your strategy?

7. What are the types of grasses on the course and how could that affect chipping and putting?

By going through this 7 Point Course Strategy Process before your rounds you'll reduce uncertainty and performance anxiety and increase confidence.

Treat all rounds the same

It's *only* you that attaches more importance to one round compared to another. Playing in a local tournament is the same physical challenge as playing in the State Open. The golf ball doesn't know what tournament it is or whether it's a putt for birdie or bogey, it's your mind that can interpret them differently and mean that you perform differently. That said, it's unrealistic to say that you shouldn't *feel* differently about a putt to win than you would a putt in practice, and that can be a good thing. As we've already discussed, higher arousal can help deepen focus and get you into Flow. But the key is to notice if you are *thinking* about them differently or adding a story to the putt you have labeled as more important.

Conversely, if you tell yourself that a golf course is easy, or that you are one of the better players, you can get sloppy. There is no such thing as a "big tournament" or a "big putt", they are all tournaments and all putts. Try to catch yourself labeling in this way and instead adopt the mindset that each shot and round is just as important as any other.

Lower Your Expectations

"Don't try to make something happen, see what happens"
— Collin Morikawa

Having high expectations is a trap that a lot of players can fall into. They might have practiced well or had a good score in a previous round, so they expect that the upcoming round will be the same. If they are in a tournament where they are one of the better players, they will expect to win or finish near the top of the leaderboard. You might be thinking that confident players *should* think this way, but as any Tour Player will tell you, there are several problems with expectations which can prevent you from being your best.

1. **An expectation is a prediction of the future – that something *should* happen**

Golf is a very unpredictable game, and you never know what is going to happen. When we expect certain desired outcomes, and the reality doesn't match up with them, it can become frustrating and get worse as the round goes on. This can affect your mood and cause you to take risks to bring yourself back in line with them. To be present (the place to be to perform your best), requires you to be fully accepting of what has happened, and what might happen in the future. If you have expectations and thoughts about what *should* happen, and then reality doesn't deliver, it can cause you to ruminate and continue to ask yourself why and how, which will keep you from being in the present.

Expectations about results can also work against you if you begin to exceed them – if you start to play better than what you expect, you might become defensive and protective, causing you to retreat and fall back in-line with your expectations. In this case, expectations can prevent you from turning a good round into a great one.

2. **Expectations add pressure**

Telling yourself that you *should* perform a certain way, and anything less will be disappointing, will no doubt add pressure. Many juniors I work with feel pressure to play perfectly which causes them to struggle even more when they don't.

3. **Expectations encourage a Fixed Mindset**

To play with freedom and have no limits to your performance, you will need a "beginner's", or "growth" mindset and be open to the possibilities, including failure.

Even at the professional level, they don't know what game they will have that day. On average, Tour players make approximately 80% of their money from 5 tournaments, so if they play in 30 in a season, it means they will only have their "A game" in 1 in 6 rounds. The rest of the time, they're having to manage their B, C and even D game and get the best out of whatever they have on that day.

Playing good golf is about expecting that there are unknowns and "uncontrollables" ahead, instead of expecting that it *should* go a certain way and that if it doesn't, something is wrong. We don't know what is going to happen – the best you can do is to be up for the challenge of every shot and be accepting of whatever the outcome might be.

When you expect things to happen, your mind is more closed off to learning, i.e., you're in a Fixed Mindset. You're better off expecting that each round will be a challenge and a learning opportunity, rather than fitting nicely into your plan for where you think your game is.

4. **Expectations and Confidence are NOT the same thing**

Having confidence is very different from having expectations. Expectations are about results – that you *will* or *should* achieve a certain score. Confidence is accepting that there will be challenges ahead but knowing that you are prepared and you have the skills to deal with them.

Be Intentional

As we discussed in Module 2, you'll need some intentions for your round that you have complete control over, rather than anything that is uncertain. Instead of being overly focused on the outcomes of the round, you're best to keep bringing your attention back to your process goals and values. Write your goals and intentions down on your Mental Scorecard or in your yardage book.

Some examples are:

- Be My Player Identity
- For each shot: Choose the best option, Visualize, Commit, Trust and Celebrate/Accept

- Be grateful for this day spending time doing something I love!

Recovery and Sleep

Being prepared also means being physically and mentally recovered and getting a good night's sleep is the best way to do this. Getting less sleep than your mind and body need each night can not only lead to mental and physical fatigue the next day, but it can cause poor focus, higher levels of the stress hormone Cortisol, anxiety, and under-performance.

The importance of sleep in an athlete's performance is vastly underestimated. Sleep expert Dr. Michael Breus says that *"Sleep recharges you physically, mentally, emotionally and spiritually. Everything we do, we do better with sleep."*

Take sleep seriously and make sure you are doing what's needed to get plenty of REM (deep) sleep. Here are some tips to do so:

1. Get to bed early enough to make sure you will get 7-8 hours of sleep
2. Don't use your computer or mobile device at least one hour before bed
3. Darken the room completely (if there are any lights at all, find a way to block them)
4. Set the temperature to cool
5. If you use your phone as an alarm and that's why it's beside your bed, consider getting an alarm

clock and leave your phone in another room. This will avoid you looking at it right before bed and first thing in the morning
6. Avoid alcohol, drinking liquids or having a big meal too close to going to bed
7. When you get into bed, calm your mind with some mindfulness practice such as breathing awareness

Sleep is so important for controlling attention, mood, mental toughness and how you feel physically. Make good sleep a habit and you'll get the best out of your mind and body each day and during your rounds.

Eat and Drink Well

Nutrition and hydration are another component of high performance which can't be overlooked.

The food and drink you put into your body will affect how you feel (physically and mentally), how well you sleep, how well you think and focus, and your energy level throughout the round.

You burn approximately 1200 calories if you walk a course carrying your bag (more in the heat), so if you're not putting at least 800 back into your body, you will start to lose energy and focus. Staying calm and thinking clearly will become more challenging. Here are my suggestions for how to eat and drink optimally before and during your rounds:

1. The evening before your round, it's important to eat a healthy meal and get a good night's sleep
2. Keep your pre-round meal light and eat 2-3 hours before playing. You can follow it up with a snack such as fruit and nuts about 30 mins before your tee time. A little coffee is fine, but not too much as this can make you jittery. Tiger's pre-round meal of choice is an egg-white omelet with vegetables. A small (brown bread) sandwich with fruit would be another good option
3. During the round, avoid the half-way hot dog and drinks that give you high blood sugar like soda or beer. The surge in insulin will make you sluggish later. Go for the healthy option of bananas, mixed nuts and granola bars and sip plenty of water

Get Your Equipment Prepared

Being prepared with the equipment you will need for your round the evening before will mean that you'll feel more relaxed in the morning. You reduce the stress from having to make decisions when time is limited. You don't want to be rushing around getting your equipment ready shortly before you have to leave for the course. Count your clubs in case any extras have made their way in there which would take you over the 14-club limit. Have your clubs, clothes, and shoes ready the evening before. Make sure your bag contains an extra glove, waterproofs, plenty of balls, tees, ball markers and a pitch-mark repairer.

Have your snacks and water ready to pop in the bag in the morning.

Your Mental Game Warm-Up

The game doesn't start on the first tee. By the time you get to hit your first shot, you should already be in your best competitive mindset and ready to play. You don't want to wait until you're several holes into your round to find it.

Sports psychologists call a mental warm up "Activation", during which, triggers can be used to:

- Create a mental, emotional and physical state
- Get you feeling confident and believing in your abilities
- Control arousal level and tension
- Reduce worry and anxiety
- Be prepared for any challenges that might arise

Here are my suggestions for a mental game warm-up that can be done in less than 20 minutes.

1. Breathe and Relax

It's normal to feel nervous before a round, which is why it's important to include exercises which prevent those nerves becoming anxiety and tension. Here's another type of meditation that can take as little as 5 minutes

Module 5: Pre-Round Preparation and Warm-Up

and focuses on quieting the mind and relaxing the body before a round:

1. Close your eyes and take a few deep breaths. Inhale deeply through your nose until your belly goes out, and exhale slowly through your mouth. On the exhale, feel your whole body relax
2. Return your breathing to normal
3. Do a body scan and notice any tension. If you notice any tension, breathe into that area, and soften it. Start with the top of your head and gradually move to your face, noticing any tension in your brow, cheeks, and jaw. Move slowly to your neck and shoulders, all the way down your arms, to the wrists and fingers. Bring awareness to the sensations in each individual part of your body. Explore it. Feel the chest and diaphragm moving with your breath. Move down each leg, thighs, calves, ankles, feet, and toes. Be aware of exactly how you feel and use your breathing to release any stress and tension. Feel your body getting more relaxed with each breath
4. Whenever you notice your attention wander from your body scan, bring it back to the breath and how your body feels

2. Be Grateful

As we discussed in Module 4, gratitude is the opposite of fear. You can't feel grateful and anxious at the same time. Let's put golf in perspective. Whatever round you are about to play, you are still going to play the game golf. You're not going to have major surgery, or anything worse than that. Think of 3 things that you are grateful for about the upcoming round, that don't have anything to do with your final score – this could be playing a good golf course, hitting some good shots, being outside in beautiful surroundings, being healthy enough to play, the people you are going to play with or the opportunity to learn more about your game. By choosing to be grateful, and staying mindful of these things throughout the round, you take some of the pressure away from having to play well to make it a success or enjoyable.

3. Visualize

> *"Mental rehearsal is every bit as important as physical rehearsal."*
> **– Phil Mickelson**

As you will know from Module 4, mental rehearsal or visualization is about creating a feeling of confidence and a positive association with what you are about to do. It embeds the possibility or success in your subconscious rather than what could go wrong or what there is to fear. Jack Nicklaus said that he attributes at least 50% of his success to having seen it in his mind before it actually happened. Muhammad Ali said he would mentally rehearse all his fights and saw himself being victorious before the actual fight.

When you are there for real, you will have more confidence and you are more likely to live into the player you have visualized.

Let's make success *more* possible by visualizing it before your rounds using this process:

1. Start by visualizing success that you have already achieved. Think of your 3 best memories in golf. Experiment with the first-person and third-person perspective (seeing it if you are playing the shots vs. as if you are on TV). What did the course look like? What was the weather like? What were you wearing? Who was there? What shots did you play? What club did you use and how did the shot feel? How did it feel afterwards? Re-live those moments as vividly as possible
2. Using the same process, visualize your success in the upcoming round. Go through your shot routine for tee shots, approaches, short game shots, long and short putts and visualize great swings and shots. E.g., see yourself on the first tee, being confident, calmly going through your Pre Shot Routine and hitting a solid shot down the center of the fairway

    Not only do you want to see yourself playing the shots but imagine the player that you want to be. You get to decide which version of you will

show up. What will your attitude, demeanor, body language and self talk be like? Visualize being your "best performing self"
3. Imagining yourself being successful on the course is not the same as expecting the round to be without any challenges. We can use mental rehearsal to prepare for adversity. Also known as "rational visualization", you can put yourself in some of the challenging situations that could arise and visualize dealing with them in the best possible way. Whether it's overcoming the feeling of nerves on the first tee, being out of position, a double bogey or a bad bounce or lie, it's important that you plan your response. Tiger said that not only does he visualize himself hitting great shots, but he also assumes that he will miss-hit some and sees himself successfully dealing with the trouble they could leave him in (he doesn't visualize mis-hitting shots). Mentally rehearse what you will do in those situations

4. Activate Your Player Identity

By this point of your training, you should be very familiar with your Player Identity, but I'd like for you to make a point to activate it before you play.

This is about clear intentions for how you will be on the course – the values and characteristics you will have.

After reading your Player Identity Statement, become that player by activating it with an action such as putting on your golf shoes or cap, playing a certain type of music, or watching videos of your model player. You can maintain it throughout your day by using key words such as *"assertive, focused and present" or combine it with a model player such as "a Calm, Tough Brooks Koepka"*.

5. Play Music

Music is a great activator of mood. Create different playlists that can activate different mental and emotional states, depending on what you feel is needed. If you need to calm yourself down and lower your nerves, you might listen to classical music. If you want to raise intensity and get yourself pumped up, you might listen to something more upbeat. Jon Rahm says he listens to rap music before playing, as the lyrics get him ready for the fight ahead. Find songs that have lyrics that align with your performance values and optimal performance state.

Having music playing while you are doing your pre-round visualizations, can connect those experiences with that music, so it becomes a trigger of that same performance state when you listen to it again.

A pre round mental warm up is an integral part of performing well in your rounds. Like a daily morning routine to start any day off well, your pre round routine will help you establish your goals and intentions, get you focused on the things that are possible for the day and have you feeling like you are prepared for anything that comes your way.

Your Physical Warm-up Routine

There are many ways to warm up your physical game, but here is a routine that many of my students have found to be effective. Stay disciplined to your warm up routine no matter how you're hitting the ball.

Putting Warm-up (15 mins)

The first thing to warm up is your putting. The subtle movement of the ball rolling will get your visualization and feel working and warm up your senses.

1. Putt to the fringe. Hit 5 putts – place them at 10-15-20-25-30ft from the fringe and putt to it, trying to get it as close as possible. The idea behind this drill is to get you focusing only on rolling the ball a certain distance, not to try and get it close to a hole. Hit one ball *only* from each spot. (3 mins)
2. Putt to a tee in the 10-20ft range. Hit 6 putts going through your full pre putt routine and vary the distance and break with each putt. Putting to a tee means that you are not judging whether you are making or missing them, anything around the tee has a chance to go in. It also narrows your focus onto a small target which will help you perceive the hole as bigger on the course. (5 mins)
3. Do the 3-4-5 Drill. Moving around a hole, hit 6 putts from 3ft, 4 putts from 4ft and 2 putts from

5ft. If you have time and you want to add some pressure, keep going until you make all 12 putts consecutively
4. Finish by hitting 5 putts into the hole from 1ft, a putt you can't miss. Notice the look and sound of the ball going into the cup

Short Game Warm-up (15 mins)

1. Pick 5 spots around the green with varying lies (tight, fluffy and rough) and distance of green to work with. Play 3 balls from each spot to a hole on the green. Notice how the ball reacts from each lie and take mental notes about how you will play each shot if you are faced with it on the course. For at least one shot from each location, go through your full Pre Shot Routine. (10 mins)
2. Play 3 long bunker shots and 3 short ones. (5 mins)

Driving Range Warm-up (20 mins)

The goal of your driving range warm up is to:

- Loosen up your muscles and be aware of any tension
- Find your Tempo
- Get your set up right (alignment and ball position)
- Get the feel for different shots you'll hit on the course
- Practice your Shot Routine and get into game mode

Here's how to achieve these goals:
Warm up your feel and find the bottom of your swing (5 balls)

In a Golf Digest interview, Jordan Spieth said that he starts his pre round driving range warm-up with a drill he calls "Walk The Dog", which helps him find his strike, tempo and feel. He says:

> *"With the first ball, I kick off a game we call Walk the Dog. I hit a little pitch, and wherever that ball stops, maybe 20 yards away, becomes the target landing spot for my next shot—and so on. Each ball runs a few yards farther than the previous, and this is how I gradually, yet quickly, work toward hitting full lob wedges. Not only does this game loosen the joints, but it also puts you in the mode of reacting to a target instead of exploring mechanical thoughts."*

Once you've hit your first ball 20 yards, try to get 4 balls slightly further than the previous ball.

Limit the number of balls (26 or 39 balls)

To avoid turning your warm-up into a practice session and making it physically taxing, limit the number of balls you hit. Colin Montgomerie says that he hits no more than 3 balls with each club, so a 39-ball warm-up. You could even limit it to 2 balls with each club (26 ball warm-up), depending on how much time you have. By doing this, it will help you get into the "one-shot mentality" that you will need on the course. It also means that you will have enough time to hit each club at least once. Put down an alignment stick and vary the targets that you aim at. With your wedges, hit a full wedge and then 2 shots that go in between yardages.

Find your rhythm and notice any tension
A consistent golf swing depends on consistent timing and your rhythm and tension are key factors in this.

As you work your way up your clubs, notice the tempo of your swing and any tension in your body. If you notice any tension, take a short break and do some diaphragmatic breathing, such as the 4-7-8 method, while focusing on the area of the tension. Make sure your grip pressure is where you want it to be.

What shots are you feeling today?
Use your warm-up time to see what shots come naturally to you that day. As humans, we are continually changing from day to day, so if that draw shape that was there a few days ago has disappeared and now you are hitting a fade, don't fight it – just play with it and find a reliable shot pattern. Too many players notice something different in their shots before a round and start panicking and go into "fix it mode" which is a bad place to be before starting a round.

Play the shots you'll need on the course
What shots will the course require you to play? As you go through your warm-up, put shots into context with those you'll need on the course.

Go through your Pre Shot Routine (5 balls)
Once you've gone through your 26 or 39 balls, hit 5 shots going through your full Pre Shot Routine. How do you want to feel as you hit each shot? It's time to get into playing mode. Finish by imagining the 1st tee shot and don't leave till you hit one that finds the fairway.

Make sure you have plenty of time to get to the first tee from the driving range, so you don't feel rushed. If you think it could be helpful, write all these shots down so you can refer to them while you are warming up.

Module 5 Exercises

Define your Pre Round Routine including what you will do the evening before and morning of your round.

Set your Process goals for each round and define your Player Identity.

Create a checklist for everything that you will need to have ready the evening before your round.

What will you visualize before your next round? Create a "visualization script" (using the process I outlined in the module), so you know exactly what you will imagine before playing.

Module 6: Post-Round Reflection

> *"I never learned anything from a match that I won."*
>
> **– Bobby Jones**

Golf is an inconsistent game by nature and scores will always fluctuate, but what's guaranteed is that every round will be a learning opportunity for long-term improvement. Too many golfers don't spend enough time reflecting on their rounds, to highlight the things that they did well, or to look at situations and shots in the round that shows them what they could do differently. This often comes back to mindset - an ego oriented "fixed" mindset is one that is more concerned about the result, the placing and how that result is perceived by others. A poor performance or a high score will cause a golfer with a Fixed Mindset to want to just forget about it. Mastery or "Growth" mindset golfers are able to be humble and look deeper into the performance to find out what was learned and what can be improved. A good Post Round Review process can help you nurture a Growth Mindset, increase your self-esteem as a player and learn from every round.

Using A Performance Journal

Studies show that writing things down in a journal is a highly effective way to reflect and learn from an experience. It gives you the opportunity to make sense of what happened during your rounds and what you were thinking and feeling in different situations. This can help you identify what about your process is working, what areas of your game needs work, and it will help you to reconcile with the round so you can move on. The kinesthetic action of writing and seeing it on the page, will make it sink in.

Even though writing on paper is most effective, most of my students use an online performance journal that shares their entries with me, which helps them stay accountable to their process and helps me learn more about them.

Use the simple Post Round Review and mental scoring system below as a template for each journal entry. You can also create separate sections of your journal for your practice and "best shot log".

A Simple Post Round Review

After a round or at the end of your day, ask yourself these simple questions:
What went well?
What was the process behind those things that you did well?

Did you act, think and behave in line with your player identity?

What did you learn and what could you have done differently?

How will you make sure you do those things differently in the future?

Let's take a look at each of these questions and why it's important to ask them.

What went well?

Whenever I ask a golfer how they played, unless they played exceptionally well, the automatic response is negative, such as: *"It would have been great if I'd not missed a short putt on the 18th"*, or *"my driving was awful"*, or *"I couldn't hole a putt today!"*. The player is compelled to tell me what they didn't do well, so the positives get buried under the negatives.

As we discussed in Module 4, when we focus too much on the negatives, we reinforce the brain's negativity bias and embed them more deeply in our memory. Instead, we want a Post Round Review that trains optimism, increases self-belief and build mental toughness.

Hence, the first step of a Post Round Review, is to highlight *all* the **positives**, such as areas of your game that were good, like putting, or aspects of your mental game, such as commitment or moving on from misses, or specific shots you were happy with. Let's anchor those highlights and write them down.

What was the process behind those things that you did well?
In order to repeat the process behind your success, you'll need to acknowledge it and highlight it. E.g., "My speed on the greens was really good because I did my lag putting drills 3 times this week", or "I felt calm and confident on the first tee because of my Pre-Round Mental Routine". Celebrate your successes and remind yourself of all the things that are leading to that success. This will build your self-esteem, reinforce your process, and have you feel more optimistic about your game. Here are some examples:

1. *Driving was great, I hit 75% of fairways – my deliberate practice and swing thought for tempo is helping*
2. *Hit 12 greens – my strategy was solid, and I had a really clear picture of each shot before I hit it*
3. *My bounceback after bad shots was very good – I pre-accepted the outcome, and focused on breathing and smiling after a miss*

Did you act, think and behave in line with your Player Identity?
With this being a goal for every round and practice session, you should have a clear definition of the values that you will uphold and the qualities you want to bring. Did you act, think and behave in line with this profile for yourself?

Module 6: Post-Round Reflection

What did you learn and what could you have done differently?

In every round there will be failures. This could be failure to pick the right shot, manage negative thoughts or execute technically. Because failure opens our eyes to what we can do differently, it is our best teacher. To grow, we need to redefine failure as a positive, not a negative. If we do so, we learn more and we become less afraid of it. If you aren't putting yourself in the positions to fail (i.e., you try to avoid it), you are missing out on the deep learning and growth that comes from being challenged.

The Post Round Review is the best time to think about what you could do differently, as it gives you a container of time to review it, so you don't dwell. It might be uncomfortable, but it's a very important part of the process of learning and finding a better way to approach those aspects of your game.

Were there certain shots that you struggled with? Moments where you were uncomfortable and didn't handle it well? Times where you picked the wrong shot or target or didn't fully commit to it?

Here's an example:

Scrambling. I got up and down twice out of 6 missed greens. I had too much fear and tension over my chip shots and found it hard to see the shot I wanted to play. Because I wasn't committed, the physical execution wasn't fluid.

How will you make sure you do those things differently in the future?

I don't recommend that you change your current practice plan based on one round, but if you notice that certain things appear frequently, you'll need to allocate time to work on them on your practice plan. I'll show you how to do this in Module 7. That said, this process in itself will bring attention to those areas of your mental game that need improvement, and through simply having them as goals for your next round you are more likely to do better with them.

By doing this simple Post Round Review:

- You will reward positive thinking, behaviors and actions, which will encourage you to do more of them in the future
- You will train yourself to seek positives and be more optimistic, instead of defaulting to the brain's negativity bias
- You will recognize the value of failure, so you'll be less fearful of it, and more accepting of it as part of the game improvement process
- You will know exactly what areas of your game you will need to train during your next goal cycle

Scoring Your Mental Game

You can dig deeper into your performance by reviewing your Mental Scorecard.

Step 1: Calculate your percentage process score using either version of the Mental Scorecard (by shot or by hole)

Step 2: Grade your overall mental performance: (i.e., A, B, C, etc.)

Step 3: Score yourself (out of 10) on these performance factors:
- Focus and commitment during your Shot Routines
- Arousal level management
- Staying present
- Self talk and Optimism
- Body language
- Acceptance of misses
- Self-awareness
- Course strategy
- Pre round preparation
- Nutrition and hydration

Total score is out of 100.

What makes a good score for these factors? Let's take a look at each one.

Focus and Commitment During Pre Shot Routines

- *How good was my focus on what I needed to do during my Pre Shot Routine?*
- *How committed was I to each shot?*

- *How good was my visualization and clarity of my intention for my shots?*
- *Did I start getting too technical with my swing and focusing on that rather than my intention?*

Arousal Level Management
- *How well did I control my heart rate?*
- *How well did I manage any tension?*
- *Which of my mental game tools were effective in controlling my arousal level?*

Staying present
- *Was I in the moment? Did I use my breathing, focus on my senses and my environment to keep me present?*
- *Was I able to bring myself into the present when I noticed negative thinking?*

Self Talk and Optimism
- *How well did I use my Self talk to motivate me and keep me process focused?*
- *Did I voice anything negative in my head or out loud?*
- *Was I able to say things to myself which reminded me of the good things that are possible? Or did I give up?*

Body Language
- *Was I aware of my body language?*
- *Did I walk like a champion and use my facial expressions to help diffuse difficult situations?*

Course strategy
- *How good was my course strategy?*
- *Did I choose the right target and the right shot? When did I not?*

Self-Awareness
- *Was I aware of any negative thinking? I.e., self-doubt, thinking about score, comparing myself to other players, what others will think, etc.*
- *Did I notice how I was feeling?*
- *What emotions surfaced during the round and why did they?*
- *How well did I do at controlling my internal state or mood?*
- *Were there specific situations that caused fear and self-doubt?*

Acceptance
- *How well did I accept misses (Post Shot Routine)?*
- *Did I respond calmly or react with high emotion?*
- *How well did I pre-accept and surrender to the possible outcome of my round and my shots?*

Pre Round Preparation
- *How well did I prepare for this golf course?*
- *Did I sleep well the night before?*
- *Did I go through my Pre Round Mental Routine?*

Nutrition and hydration
- *Did I eat properly and hydrate the evening and morning of the round?*

- *Did I feel tired at any point in the round?*
- *Did I remember to eat snacks and sip water?*

By going through the exercise of scoring your mental game, you'll increase your self-awareness on the golf course and be able to respond most effectively to keep you in your optimal performance state.

Stats to Record

If you really want to become as good as you can be, you'll need to track data for your rounds. You need to know what your strengths and opportunities are, by looking at your stats. Spending 10-20 mins *after* each round and entering them into a stat tracking system is well worth the time. Without stats, your practice won't be as effective, and you won't be able to set the right goals. There are plenty of good stat tracking apps/tools available that will help you analyze your game and give you your "Strokes Gained" numbers for all shots and distances. Your most negative Shots Gained numbers are the areas of your game you will need to prioritize.

Stat tracking systems are good as you can see your stats over a period of several rounds, rather than being reactive to your performance in the previous round.

Further Questions:
You can dig deeper into each aspect of the game by asking yourself some additional questions.

Putting
How good was my green reading?
Were my misses due to line or speed?
Was I fully committed to every putt?
Where was my focus over the ball?
Was there any negative chatter while over the ball?

Short game
Did I choose the right shots around the greens and was I confident in my execution?

Was I connected to my landing zone, the trajectory and release and did I see it in my mind?

Did I have a sense of the look, feel and sound of the shots?

As you will have gathered by now, your reflection and evaluation of your performance is how we learn, build confidence, and refine the plan to improve performance, which is why it's important to spend the time doing it.

In the next module, we'll take a look at how you can use this information to set goals and take your game to the next level.

Module 6 Exercises

Practice with the Mental Scorecard

Buy a blank journal and start journaling after each round and practice session using the template in the module

Module 7: Planning and Executing

"Time is the only thing you can't buy more of. I mean, I can buy anything I want, but I can't buy time."
— **Warren Buffet**

In Module 1, I asked you what your vision for your game is and the meaning behind it. I'd like you to revisit that vision for your future often. Reminders of who you want to become, what you want to achieve and why, will provide ongoing motivation to spend your valuable time on the things that are most important to you.

Although it's important to have a vision, your goals are obviously *not* going to happen just by thinking about them. Assuming that higher performance is your goal, you have a daily opportunity to make small gains in mental, technical, and physical skills, which add up to big gains over time. Dave Brailsford, the coach of the Tour de France winning British cycling team, calls long-term success: *"The aggregation of marginal gains."*

In order to maximize and dedicate our limited and precious time to our long-term goals, we need to create an effective plan, and work that plan daily. A plan takes decision making, emotions and stress out of the daily process as you will know with 100% certainty what you need to do.

There are many different theories and systems that you can use to set goals and be productive, but this is the one that I have found to be most effective for all personality types.

The Goal Setting and Achievement Process

"Excellence is not a destination; it is a continuous journey that never ends."
— Brian Tracy, motivational speaker and author

We introduced goal types in Module 2 when we discussed Outcome and Process goals. Outcome goals can be broken down further into "External" and "Internal" goals. Let's take a look at some examples:

What Motivates YOU?

External	Internal
Winning a Specific Tournament	Being more Focused
	Having a Strong Work Ethic
Having a High Status In The Game	Building Confidence
Impressing others	Improving Scoring Average
Winnning Prize Money	Performing Better Under Pressure
Collecting Awards	Learning how to control your Mind
Rankings	Ongoing Skill Development

External Goals

External (or "Extrinsic") goals are called such because they are goals for what your progress will lead to outside of yourself E.g., how many tournaments you win, how you will be perceived by others, how much money you will make, or what your ranking will be.

Is your goal to win the Club Championship, an AJGA or USGA tournament or even The Masters? The first question to ask yourself is "why is that?" Is it because you want status or respect from others? That you believe that you will be a happier and better person once you have achieved it? Or is it because you love competing and developing your skills, and winning a tournament like that would represent your growth as a player?

External goals are helpful if:

- They push you to work harder. Tiger Woods pushed himself with the goal of beating Jack's record of 18 majors. Michael Phelps thought about the Olympic gold medals he wanted to win every day
- There is a mastery purpose behind them - that the goal represents the skill level that you want to reach, and it tells you what skills you need to improve to get there

However, there are downsides to external goals. Too much emphasis on external goals can cause you to lose focus on your journey of continuous improvement, which never ends. External goals should be a pointer and never more important than the journey itself.

If everything you do is geared towards an external goal you can easily get critical, disheartened, and lose motivation if you don't see progress towards it. External goals can easily cause you to second guess your strategy and process. The stress of measuring yourself against an external goal can rob you of being present and the mental energy needed to be your best every day and to enjoy the journey. Sure, the journey will have ups and downs (and never be stress free), but to navigate them successfully requires you to be as patient, disciplined and objective as possible.

If we take a round of golf as a representation of your journey, should the success and satisfaction of the game be solely about what score you have on your card at the end? If it is, it can cause you stress and possible disappointment, a loss of focus on process, and you'll miss out on the joy and learning to be found in the experience.

Some players tend to think that they will be happier when they've achieved an external goal, and for that reason, they are in a constant state of striving, and *only* see success as scores, trophies, and wins, etc.

Instead of chasing results and the feeling that you think that will bring, I prefer what meditation teacher Jon Kabat-Zinn calls "non-striving," where you are fully present to what you are doing, you're not constantly doing something to achieve a future outcome or to feel better. When all your energy is in the present, you are giving 100% of yourself to what you are doing *now* which opens the possibilities.

As hard as you try, you might never reach an external goal, and if you do, what next? There can be a hollowness and an anti-climax. There have been Tour players who have set the goal of winning a major and then when they achieved it, they didn't know what to do next and spent the next few years going backwards, instead of continuing to grow. When we define success as being black and white before a journey begins or label ourselves as being this or that in relation to that goal, it can prevent us from having the freedom to fully express ourselves and to go as far as we can. I would prefer a student of mine to have the long-term goal "to become a player that is capable of winning majors", rather than the goal "to win a major".

I suggest you think about any External goals during two select windows –goal setting/planning and daily visualization. During the rest of the goal achievement process you should focus on "internal" goals or "doing the work".

Happiness and high performance aren't found in external goals, it comes from inside you, which is why Internal goals should be your primary focus throughout the journey. Winning is a biproduct of the completion of Internal goals and developing a deeper mental, emotional, and physical connection with what you do.

Internal Goals

Internal ("Intrinsic") goals are more about the player you will become and the skills and values you will cultivate on your journey. Internal goals place more value on making progress within *your* game, rather than how it stacks up to others or what you achieve with it. With Internal goals, *you* are your own measure of success, not rankings, placings or trophies won.

These goals are within your control and will have you focusing on being the best version of yourself every day. Who is the player you want to become? What skills and values does he or she have?

Once you have established your Internal goals, you will need to convert them into tasks or "process goals", allocate precious time to them, and be accountable for doing them. Success and satisfaction are about doing the daily work as you know it represents progress.

Taking Inventory and Setting Your Goals

To set the best internal or skill development goals, you will need to take an honest inventory of your game, so you can clearly see the biggest opportunities to become the player that you want to be.

A CEO of a large company would look at all the departments of the business and evaluate them to find out which are performing well, and which are underperforming. In a similar way, we need to look at your strengths and "opportunities" so you continue to do those things you do well and improve in those areas where you can do better.

For this part of the goal setting process, I'd like you to print out the "Goal Setting Sheet" which you can find on my website along with all the other resources and worksheets at: https://golfstateofmind.com/module-resources-email/

How to Use the Goal Setting Sheet
1. Write in your Vision or "Dream goal"
2. Write in your Target Handicap in 1 year from now. This is going to depend on how much time you can invest, but it's better to be conservative and achieve it, than unrealistic and under achieve it
3. For each of the 3 skill categories of the game: Mental, Technical and Physical (for simplicity we'll add "tactical" to "mental"), we're going to decide on 2 areas (a primary and secondary) to work on over the next 8-12 weeks or "short-term goal cycle". The purpose of this is to get you focused on 2 aspects within each skill area that will have the biggest impact on improving your performance, instead of trying to work on many things and not getting better at any of them. Here's how to decide on your primary and secondary goals for each area:

Setting Technical Goals
To set technical goals, you will need to do an evaluation of your game and ideally, you'll have access to stats from your last 10-20 rounds.

Many stat tracking tools will give you comparable detailed stats (to your target handicap) but for illustration purposes, take a look at the following table:

Module 7: Planning and Executing

	Fairway Acc.	GIR%	Putts/ Hole	Scrambling	Sand Save	Driving Distance
Scratch (72 avg. or lower)	56%	69%	1.6	59%	63%	250 Yards
72-75	53%	62%	1.72	44%	57%	249 Yards
75-80	51%	52%	1.79	32%	39%	235 Yards
80-85	48%	41%	1.87	22%	24%	222 Yards
85-90	45%	31%	1.93	15%	17%	208 Yards
90-95	43%	23%	2.01	10%	9%	196 Yards
95-100	41%	19%	2.07	8%	6%	184 Yards
100-105	41%	14%	2.13	5%	3%	171 Yards
105-110	43%	11%	2.17	4%	1%	158 Yards
110-115	39%	10%	2.22	4%	1%	154 Yards
115-120	42%	8%	2.34	3%	1%	145 Yards

Let's take the example of a 12 handicap golfer looking to become an 8 in the next year. This player would reference the table to see which aspect of their technical game is furthest away from the 75-80 scoring average. If he or she has a similar profile to this but only gets up and down 15% of the time after they miss a green, then this would be the area to focus on. For this player, a primary goal could be scrambling % from 20 yards and in, and a secondary goal could be Putts made % from 10-15 feet (no need for specific number targets).

Many Tour players use the Strokes Gained approach that shows a player how many strokes they are gaining or losing to "the field" from any distance from the hole. With more detailed stats, our 10 handicapper would know if it was the proximity of their chips and pitches, or whether it's their make % of the par putt, that is the reason they don't shoot more rounds in the 70s.

Some coaches might argue that you should put a target stat to each area of the game that you want to improve, e.g., to improve scrambling % to 40%, but I believe that once you know what you need to work on, doing the work is the only thing you need to be focused on. You don't need the distraction of what your numbers are during that goal period. If you do the work, you are making progress towards a lower scoring average.

After the 8-12 week period, you can do another review of your stats and set new short-term goals.

Setting Goals for the Mental and Physical Game

Obviously the mental and physical game is not as "measurable" and you won't have stats for them, but you will still need to know what you need to improve and set goals for them. Taking a look at your mental game requires some honest reflection and for you to determine where you are now mentally in relation to the player you want to become.

Let's revisit your Player Identity. You should have a clear idea of who you want to be during every round and practice session i.e., your mindset, how you want to feel, what you will focus on, how you will behave and deal with challenges.

Are you being that person? If not, which of those attributes of your Player Identity are you lacking? Consider adding one of these attributes as a short-term goal, e.g., being more disciplined, more patient, more grateful and optimistic, etc.

To assess where you are with each of the mental game performance factors, you can score yourself out of 10 for the following (you'll notice this is the same scoring system as the Post Round Review):

- Focus and commitment during your Shot Routines
- Staying present
- Self Talk
- Body language
- Acceptance
- Self-awareness of thoughts/feelings/emotions
- Course strategy
- Arousal level management
- Pre round preparation
- Nutrition and hydration

Your scores out of 10 can tell you what you should add as an internal goal. E.g., if you gave yourself a 3 out of 10 for Self Talk, then this could be one of your goals. For the "physical" game (strength, fitness, sleep and nutrition), find a similar way to assess and set Internal goals.

Process Goals or "The Tasks"

Now you know what skills you need to work on, we need to figure out what *to do* to develop them. We need to determine the tasks, or "process goals" to take us to the next level.

The simplest example of a process goal is the allocation of time to do something e.g., *"I will spend*

3 hours on my short game this week". That goal is achieved once you've spent 3 hours on your short game whatever the outcome of the session.

You are doing it; a) because you enjoy hitting short game shots and learning new ways to play them, and b) You know that by spending time on your short game you should improve it (although the type of drills you do, how focused you are and the effort you put in during the sessions will affect the rate of improvement).

There are 3 places where you can work on your game: at HOME, at PRACTICE and on the golf COURSE. Below each place, I've added the types of practice you can do there.

HOME	**PRACTICE**	**COURSE**
Meditation	Driving range	Player Identity
Visualization	Short Game	Process Goals
Affirmations	Putting	Routines
Journal		
Reading/Listening		
Gym/Fitness		

Create A Two Week Plan ("The System")

"Planning places effort, where effort is most needed."

– **Coach John Wooden**

We are going to break your short-term goals into 2 week "Sprints".

Module 7: Planning and Executing

1. Print out the **2 Week Plan** (which you'll find as a link on the resources page on my website: https://golfstateofmind.com/module-resources-email/)
2. Estimate how much time you can dedicate to the 3 practice places in each of the next 2 weeks. E.g., HOME: 6 hours/week, PRACTICE: 3 hours/week, COURSE: 1 round/week
3. Write in all the activities you will do each week for the next 2 weeks, to fill that time i.e., the drills, exercises and games you will do. You can reference the Golf State of Mind Practice Book to decide on what specific drills you will do

Give a little more time to your primary goal compared to your secondary goal.

Remember, success with these tasks has nothing to do with the outcome, process goals are achieved by the *doing*.

A good plan takes away decision making and any possible barriers to putting in the work, so that you know exactly what you need to do. If we bring an outcome into it or more qualitative goals, it can cause us to compare ourselves against them which in turn can cause anxiety, stress and a loss of motivation to put in the work (this doesn't include the time during "Performance Practice" where we intentionally use the outcome of a drill to create pressure and increase intensity).

A simple example of following a plan or formula is like going to the gym with a clear list of all the exercises you will do with the number of reps, rather than going there and not knowing what you are going to do. It's much easier to get started and keep it going with goals that are simply about the doing, not the outcome. After a short while, these activities will become habits and will be easier and easier to do.

Get Your Tasks in The Calendar!
Once you've decided on your process goals, we need to get them into the calendar and protect that time. Use the calendar on the 2-week plan to confirm *when* you will do these tasks. You can then block time in your digital calendar and have reminders set.

James Clear, author of "Atomic Habits", tells us that time-based cues are important in developing strong habits i.e., try to do certain tasks at the same time each day and on certain days of the week e.g.

- every Tuesday evening at 6pm I do short game practice
- I meditate every morning at 6:30am
- I do 50 Super Speed reps Wednesday and Friday at noon
- I journal every evening at 9:30pm before bed

A goal setting example:
When a player tells me that their goal for this season is to "win the Club Championship," an external goal, I advise them to immediately turn it into internal and process goals. I don't think that the goal of winning the

Club Championship is a poor choice of goal, provided that the winning is more about becoming that player (internal) than the title itself (external). Too much focus on that championship itself is likely to interfere with the skill development needed to achieve it and add pressure to that particular tournament.

The first step is to think about the score they would likely need to shoot to win the Club Championship and to evaluate if that is possible within the time they have available. Once we've established that it's possible, we need to look deeper into their game to figure out what specific areas they need to improve and focus on these areas for the next 8-12 weeks. Throughout this process, no further thought needs to be given to the possible outcome of winning the Club Championship – they will simply work the plan or "trust the process" and let the outcome take care of itself.

Let's take a look at the Internal goals or skills the player must improve so we can set to achieve their goal of winning the Club Championship.

8-12 week Technical Goals:
- Primary: Improve Scrambling
- Secondary: Improve putting average from 10-15 feet

8-12 week Mental Goals:
- Primary: Improve mindset
- Secondary: Better Self Talk

8-12 week Physical Goals:
- Primary: Core strength
- Secondary: Improvement in Club Head Speed

PROCESS GOALS:
Home/Gym (6 hours/wk):
- Positive Affirmations and Getting into My Best Mindset daily (3 mins, 5 x per week)
- Meditation (10 mins, 5 x per week)
- Visualization (3 mins, 5 x per week)
- Writing in my Performance Journal (10 mins, 5 x per week)
- Go through my Pre Shot Routine in the backyard (5 mins, 4 x week)
- Super speed training (10 mins x 2 per week)
- Reading/Listening to the Golf State of Mind program (10 mins per day x 5 per week)
- Strength Workout in the Gym 2 x 1 hour per week

Practice (3 hours/wk):
- Short game practice (1.5 hours)
  - Par 18 game
  - 3 Spots Chipping game
  - Short Game Leapfrog
- Putting Practice (1 hour)
  - 5-50 drill
  - The Birdie Maker
  - Distance Control Ladder
- Driving Range Practice (0.5 hours):

- 26 shots in 30 mins. Hit 2 shots with each of my 13 clubs, so 26 total shots, hitting to different targets and going through my full Pre Shot Routine

Course (1 round/wk):
Go through all routines, but pay special attention to:
- Pre Round Routine: Getting into a winning mindset
- Better Self Talk
- Decide on use of Self Talk before playing
- Awareness of my thinking
- Process based or positive self talk

Here are some other strategies that can help you succeed:
What are the Obstacles to achieving your process goals?
"Winners anticipate, losers react."
–Tony Robbins

It's one thing to come up with a great plan and have the best intentions, but as you know yourself better than anyone else knows you, think about the obstacles that could stand in the way of you getting the work done (and making it focused work), and determine what you will do to overcome them E.g., if you know that practicing with your phone in your pocket causes you to lose focus and you start scrolling social media and reading messages, then you would be better off leaving your phone in the car.

Accountability

Research shows that accountability is a big factor in achieving goals. To be more accountable, share your goal sheet and plan with someone else, so they know what you are working towards, how you are going to do it and by when you will do it. All of my students share their goals with me throughout the coaching process. After every 8-12 week period we set new short-term goals and the student is responsible for doing the weekly exercises we set. Studies show that when you share your goals, you increase your commitment and effort level towards them. When you are only accountable to yourself, it can be easy to have that *"I'll do it tomorrow"* attitude.

Reward your progress

Research shows that we get a dopamine boost when we check off completed tasks. Print off your plan, put it somewhere you will see it every day (there's no point setting goals that get quickly forgotten about because you don't remind yourself of them) and then physically put a line through the tasks when you've done them. Alternatively, you can write your daily goals out on a card that you put on your desk and cross each task off as you go.

At the end of each goal setting period, revisit your stats. Did you make progress? If you did, celebrate it! Reinforce those behaviors that are helping you be more successful. If you didn't, why was that? Figure out what you need to change to make it a more productive and successful next 8-12 weeks and repeat the goal setting process.

Using Visualization in Goal Setting

"Seeing" yourself becoming the player you want to be takes you closer to it for the following reasons:

1. It increases motivation and engagement. When you can clearly see where you want to go, the player you want to become and how it will feel to get there, it can raise your energy levels and help you put in extra effort each day
2. It creates familiarity with your goal. If you've seen yourself over and over again doing something successfully, there will be less uncertainty and fear around it. You are programming (or "priming") your subconscious mind to feel positive about it, so when you are there for real, you'll be less overwhelmed by it
3. It's a way to connect more deeply with your "why?" I.e., Now that you've seen it and experienced it, ask yourself what it is that you love about this goal? Will you be fulfilled when you achieve that goal?
4. You can anticipate the challenges ahead and how you will deal with them. The path to success is never an easy one. If we *only* visualize achieving our goals, it can trick the subconscious into thinking that we have already achieved them, which can *decrease* motivation and effort. Achieving your goals will require you to overcome fears and challenges and put in hard work. For this reason, you must visualize the work ahead and the obstacles that you will face

Visualizing you achieving your goals isn't about imagining the adoration that you will get or having the feeling of being better than anyone else. It's about seeing the manifestation of all the work you've done and skills you will have developed.

Visualization of Your Player Identity

What are the characteristics of the player you want to become? What thinking and behaviors will you need to change to become that player? Do you need to be tougher in the face of adversity? Calmer under pressure? More focused? More grateful? Smile more?

Visualizing yourself with these characteristics can take you closer to developing them every day.

Visualization to Improve Technique

Neuroscience has shown that athletes don't need to be physically training to practice their movement. Golfers can ingrain new movement patterns and train their swings simply by using their imagination.

Dr. Amishi Jha says in her book Peak Mind, *"Brain imaging research shows that mental rehearsal activates the motor cortex similar to the way that actual physical movement does, exercising and strengthening neural networks similar to the way that physical exercise does for muscles."*[4]

If you know the desired movement pattern or changes to your swing you would like to make, then you can work on making those changes by closing your

---

[4] The Peak Mind, Amishi P. Jha

eyes and imagining the sensations (look and feel) of the movement.

Visualization Exercises:
For Goal Setting:

1. Write down 5 milestone moments in the achievement of your long-term goals, such as the final hole to win a championship, or the playing level you will reach
2. For each milestone moment, including the achievement of your long-term goals, make it as vivid as possible: I.e., how it will look, feel and sound to achieve that success. Imagine the weather, what you're wearing, the golf course and how confident you will look and feel. Imagine the feeling of being presented with the trophy
3. Spend one minute visualizing each moment
4. Once you have created your "goal script", familiarize yourself with it and use it as a weekly visualization

For your Player Identity:
Write out your player identity and put a visual image to each of those characteristics i.e., imagine times when you will be focused, disciplined, accepting, etc.

To Improve Technique:
1. Close your eyes and visualize the swing/technical change you are working on

2. Imagine the look, feel and sound of the swing/shot
3. Hit a variety of different short game shots and putts
4. Do this daily for 5 minutes

Golf and The Parallels with Life

I believe that the reason we love the game of golf so much is because it's a "mirror for life". Within each round we get to test our life skills, without any real-life consequences. Although what you shoot is not a reflection of the person you are, how you handle yourself on the golf course is. How you deal with the challenges and the ups and downs, is very much the same. Golf is a difficult game, as is the game of life, but the rewards are there with ongoing reflection, hard work, discipline and adopting a good mindset. With the right approach, the golf course can be a practice ground for self-development to become a better person on and off the course.

As I said at the beginning of this book, all the mental coaching I do can be applied to any field. To become successful in golf, we need to develop the same mental skill sets that we need to be successful in anything we do, such as:

Being able to focus and stay present
This is increasingly more challenging in the high-tech world we live in with all the connection we have to others and sources of information and entertainment.

Being able to give more of yourself to the present moment without being distracted, is a skill that will help us in golf and in life.

Being able to overcome setbacks
In golf and life, there will always be unexpected setbacks and stressful times. Your ability to deal with adversity will be key to your success in both. Can you keep emotions out of your decisions and approach problems with objectivity and a Growth Mindset? There will always be doubts, but you will have to be strong enough to ignore that little voice in your head telling you that you're not good enough or that you won't succeed. Staying strong in the face of adversity is what separates success and underperformance in both golf and life.

Being honest with yourself
Taking the time to self-reflect and take a good honest look at yourself is what all top performers are able to do. What is it that you truly want? Where are you now? What do you need to do to get to where you want to go? These are all key questions that you need to take the time to ask yourself and figure out the answers to for golf and life.

Setting long and short-term goals
Giving yourself targets with timeframes and a clear plan of action is an effective way to keep you progressing in anything you do. Identify your long and short-term goals and figure out what you need to do daily to take you closer to them.

Having a positive attitude and being grateful
All top performers in any field have a positive attitude and optimism. You can't be successful by being negative and pessimistic. Set a good tone for each day by being grateful and optimistic about the possibilities. At the end of each day, choose to focus on the positive experiences you had, before looking at what you could have done better.

The real value of the game of golf is not trophies or scores, but what it teaches us about ourselves and the life skills that we can develop to become better people and live more fulfilling lives.

Thank you for reading!
As you play and score yourself by your mental game and become more aware of the areas you need to improve, please revisit the relevant modules to work on them.

I also coach many golfers remotely and I have students all over the world. If this is something of interest to you, please feel free to contact me by email at david@golfstateofmind.com and we can set up a time discuss your game and my current availability.

Printed in Great Britain
by Amazon